Producing Jazz

Producing Jazz

The Experience of an
Independent Record Company

Herman Gray

TEMPLE UNIVERSITY PRESS
Philadelphia

Temple University Press, Philadelphia 19122
Copyright © 1988 by Temple University. All rights reserved
Published 1988
Printed in the United States of America

LIBRARY OF CONGRESS
Library of Congress Cataloging-in-Publication Data

Gray, Herman, 1950–
Producing jazz: the experience of an independent record company / Herman Gray.
        p.   cm.
Discography: p.
Bibliography: p.
Includes index.
ISBN 0-87722-574-5
1. Sound recording industry—United States. 2. Theresa Records (Firm) I. Title.
ML3790.G74 1988
        338.7'617899—dc19   88-15925
CIP
MN

For my parents

CONTENTS

CONTENTS

PREFACE

I originally got interested in independent cultural production as a graduate student in sociology at the University of California, Santa Cruz. Having worked as a jazz announcer at various community and public radio stations I was curious about the organization of work, and its significance, at small independent and counter-cultural organizations. As a student of sociology and longtime jazz enthusiast I was interested in the various activities involved in the creation and production of jazz as an expression of cultural resistance.

If jazz is essentially a music of black American affirmation and resistance, which I continue to believe it is, then what are the social, economic, aesthetic, and political negotiations required to present it, and still maintain these qualities? Are the qualities inherent in the music? Perhaps they derive from the circumstances of its creation and production? And are the values and orientations out of which jazz's affirmation comes shared by musicians, entrepreneurs, fans, and others involved in the music? How is it expressed and what happens to these values under the conditions of cultural production in American capitalism? If jazz truly expresses affirmative and resistant qualities, then maybe the social organization and activity necessary to create and market it are also different from mainstream commercial operations.

These interests were eventually consolidated and given form when I settled on a study of cultural creation and production in jazz. Problems of accessibility and size steered me away from large corporate recording companies. I was also less interested in major companies because they were already well represented in much of the sociological literature on the American recording industry. Perhaps most urgently, I was driven to see if the small independent record company was or might potentially be the repository of alternative cultural practice.

My contact with Theresa Records, an independent jazz record label located in the San Francisco Bay area, was a rather fortunate coincidence. I met Kazuko, one of the co-owners, in 1980 at a jazz conference, where we shared ideas and impressions of the conference and the general state of jazz. She invited me to sit in on a Theresa recording session. During the months that followed, I continued to talk with her about the music business, particularly her experience in it. I attended recording and mixing sessions more frequently, which led to my deeper involvement with the company and ultimately my decision to do a more careful study of its experience. Over the course of fifteen months I observed and, to a limited extent, participated in various company activities, attending meetings and talking to musicians, artists, and others associated with the company. I was also present at concerts and generally "hung out" with Kazuko and her partner, Allen, observing all phases of their work. I occasionally helped move equipment, offered suggestions and opinions when they were solicited, and generally helped around the company whenever I could. My direct involvement with the company lasted for three years.

This book is not so much about my experience with Theresa as it is an account of how and why an independent company like Theresa survives in the contemporary music business. The company was formed in 1975 by Allen, who, after failing to secure a recording contract with a major firm, decided to form his own label. As an independent label Theresa did not distribute its own records, but depended on a national network of independent distributors. Stylistically, Theresa's public musical identity was organized around a small group of musicians including Pharoah Sanders, Nat Adderley, John Hicks, and George Coleman. Stylistically these musicians all had strong musical ties to the"straight-ahead" acoustic musical stylings of the bebop and post-bebop periods of the 1950s and 1960s. The company maintained an artist roster of nine musicians.

Theresa's music appealed to the loyal and musically knowledgeable jazz enthusiast. Letters to the company suggested that its fans, who were located in the United States, Europe, and Japan, closely followed the career of the company as well as the careers of its major artists. When possible Theresa's record buyers attended concerts and performances by Theresa artists.

By 1987 Theresa Records had released a total of twenty-two records. Record sales from its modest catalogue varied from artist to artist, but on the average sales remained in the range of 7,000 to 8,000 records per unit. One record, *Journey to the One* approached sales of 10,000 units and for a period appeared on *Billboard's* "Top Selling Jazz LPs" chart. The company's sales were slow and steady, continuing over long periods rather than achieving huge sales in short periods.

Together with Allen, Kazuko owned and managed Theresa Records. In her mid-forties, with a Ph.D. in chemistry, Kazuko was calm and soft-spoken, and her organized approach to her work and the company was one of her obvious imprints on the company. Although a dedicated music enthusiast, Kazuko got involved in the music business unintentionally. Before joining Theresa full time, Kazuko had devoted her time to her developing career as a research cell biologist. After meeting Allen, she sat through several recording sessions and appeared on some of Theresa's early records as the assistant producer. This participation eventually led to financial investment and a formal partnership in the company. Although primarily involved in daily administration and management, Kazuko also participated in all phases of the production and promotion of records.

Allen, a tall, graying man in his fifties, was energetic but easy-going. He too was soft-spoken and seemed to get along especially well with musicians. Like Kazuko, Allen had a Ph.D. in chemistry and, until he became involved in the record business full time, had been a successful polymer chemist. (He met Kazuko through their musical rather than professional interests.) His involvement in the record business developed through his work as a trumpet player in the One Mind Experience, a San Francisco area band. In fact, it was Allen's frustration with his cool reception from major record companies when he tried to secure a recording contract for the One Mind Experience that led him to form Theresa Records.

Paul, the other major member of the company, divided his time between Theresa and his own career as a composer/pianist. As a producer, arranger, and editor Paul helped shape the final sound of Theresa's music. He also handled the shipping and receiving duties, which involved getting records to distributors and radio stations. Although younger and sometimes less available than either Kazuko or Allen, Paul was, nevertheless, central to the direction and sound of Theresa Records. In addition to Paul, Allen, and Kazuko various other

people—office managers, artists, consultants, and writers—
were involved with the company.

After completing the original study, in 1983, I moved from
California to New England. That year, the organizational and
economic pressures of running a small independent record
company seemed to weigh heavily on Allen and Kazuko. On
one of the last occasions that we spoke that year, after an
exciting evening of music by one of Theresa's artists' Allen
expressed a mix of pessimism, realism, commitment, and
hope about the future of Theresa. He noted, rather hopefully,
"We'll give it a try . . . ," continuing, "If this music doesn't
sell as good as it is and as well known as this band is, then
I'll think about getting out." Allen's comments convey the
mixture of uncertainty and conviction that characterizes the
experiences of many people involved in independent jazz labels.

Some three years later, the opportunity to publish this
account of Theresa's experience required that I bring the company's story up to date. I wanted a better feel for how Theresa
survived and at what cost. I returned to Theresa in the summer
of 1986. In the three years since I'd left California, Allen and
Kàzuko had remained the primary members of the company,
but Allen's role in the company had expanded and Kazuko's
decreased. Allen had assumed more responsibility for the day-
to-day operation of the company and he had taken over (from
Paul) the responsibilities for distribution and promotion. In
addition Allen also continued to serve as the primary producer, screening artists, listening to tapes, and maintaining a
presence in the recording studio. Kazuko had returned to the
lab and her research career, but she continued to manage
Theresa's general and financial records and coordinate the

packaging and release of new material. Paul no longer lived in California, but when possible he continued to help out as a general producer and editor.

This, then, is the story of how one small jazz record company survived and what their survival means for alternative music and culture. The account describes some of the circumstances, joys, motivations, frustrations, and constraints that the owners, musicians, and fans face in the documentation and presentation of jazz.

In love for the music, intellectual direction, encouragement, and friendship, many people contributed to the realization of this book. Hardy Frye, Todd Gitlin, and John I. Kitsuse, my dissertation committee at the University of California, Santa Cruz, provided important intellectual direction and support. They along with Howard Becker and Michael Useem listened patiently to my ideas. At a very early stage in the project, Marcia Millman encouraged my immersion in the world of the jazz record industry.

Davia Nelson and Nikki Silva, two of the best radio producers I know, helped gather valuable information about feminist independent recording labels. "Genial" Johnny Simmons, program director at KUSP-FM, Santa Cruz, also shared interview materials and talk about record distribution and blues independents. It was while doing a weekly jazz program at KUSP-FM that I first heard Theresa's music.

Several musicians and people involved in the jazz music business contributed to my understanding of the recording industry. Stanley Cowell talked with me about his experiences at Strata-East Records. Dr. Herb Wong at BlackHawk Records and Orrin Keepnews at Landmark Records took time from their busy schedules to talk about their involvement in the jazz music business. Duncan Browne at Rounder Distribution made real the world of independent record distribution.

I am especially indebted to Allen, Kazuko, Paul, Pharoah Sanders, Nat Adderley, John Hicks, Walter Booker, and other members of the Theresa family who tolerated my presence in their very personal work and creative spaces. They answered my questions and made me feel welcome with their spirit, creativity, and music.

James Reid, Modupe Smith, Linda Compton, Carsbia Anderson, Cynthia Rauf, Davia Nelson, David Wellman, and John Kitsuse along with Hardy Frye and his family all made my stay in California during the summer of 1986 special through friendship, support, good food, and lots of music. That summer Troy Duster and Hardy Frye provided a place to work at the Institute for the Study of Social Change in Berkeley. A research grant from my home institution, Northeastern University, made that summer's research possible.

Janet Francendese, my editor at Temple University Press, saw the sparkle of Theresa's story early and believed in it. She is a capable and supportive editor who cared enough about the music to ask the right kinds of questions. Thanks also to Doris Braendel, Managing Editor at Temple University Press, whose meticulous attention to detail considerably strengthened this book. My wife Kreta was there through it all and still enjoys Theresa's music. This book is better because of her love and support.

Producing Jazz

O N E

INTRODUCTION

Music, you see, is an art and it has to always be treated that way. I'm talking about creativity, you can't talk about no fucking numbers—I'm sorry. The trouble with the record industry is that people are always saying "What did he do last? What's his sales?" Well shit! The big record companies, between you and I, put the little companies out of business. But the little companies developed people like me. The little companies could take an artist and grow with the artist and let him experiment—if it weren't for experiment, Ray Charles as we know him today wouldn't exist.

Ray Charles (quoted in Guralnick 1986: 69)

The popular music industry includes hundreds of "little" independent recording companies like Theresa Records that depend on a network of independent distributors to get their products to the public. Like Ray Charles, many artists begin their careers with small independent labels before moving on to larger labels. Where the larger major companies are publicly held corporations, small firms are privately owned and financed. Independent labels release far fewer records annually and maintain a smaller catalogue of products. Independents collectively control less than 20 percent of the popular music market and often they focus on more specialized music such as jazz, gospel, rap, folk, and women's music.

In the last ten years hundreds of small record companies have

come into being as a result of . . . changes in the recording industry. Many of these labels such as Rounder, Flying Fish, . . . Olivia, Ridge Runner, and Inner City started by offering types of music not offered by major labels.
These small labels operate with budgets and sales expectations greatly scaled down from the big business projects of the majors. Most involve no more than three people overseeing the entire operation, even when as many as twenty-five albums are released per year. Their sales expectations may range from 5,000 to 50,000 records per release. (Rapaport 1979: 2)

The focus on smaller, more specialized audiences, for these companies, means that the financial threshold to break even is much lower than for large major companies. Independents can sell fewer records to a more predictable (stable) audience and still remain in business. Many independent companies operate with recording budgets that average between $15,000 and $30,000 per project. Low budgets and small but stable markets allow these companies to profit with sales of less than 3,000 units per record (Rapaport 1979).

Because of their size, stable markets, and specialized music, these labels, as Ray Charles notes, experiment more often and take musical chances with their artists. This gives them greater room to explore unconventional and innovative music that may be too risky financially and aesthetically for larger firms. New and less well-known artists, those with a small following, and those who want to exercise musical control over their work typically record on independent labels.

In contrast to independents are the major recording corporations, like CBS, Warner Inc., Polygram, RCA, Thorn, and MCA, that dominate the recording industry. Arista,

A&M, Motown, and Fantasy, among others, form a second tier of major companies that are similar to the majors in every respect except for size. In some cases, they rely on the large major labels for distribution or they provide distribution service for small independents. For instance, in 1987 *Billboard* reported the following label consolidations and distribution deals for jazz labels: Fantasy made deals with Pablo, Prestige, Riverside, and Contemporary; Polygram Records with ECM and Verve; MCA with GRP, Impulse!, Zebra, and Cranbary (Keepnews 1987). In each case these deals provided the smaller independents with greater market access and visibility.

Together major corporations and large major independents dominate the popular music market. Major companies produce records, tapes, videos, and compact discs across musical genres and styles. Many of the most popular jazz recording artists—Miles Davis, Wynton Marsalis, David Sanborn, Herbie Hancock, Bob James, Grover Washington Jr.—record with major labels. It is this group of labels that Ray Charles had in mind when he said that they are driven by the numbers—the pressure to maintain sales, hits, and profits.

In the last twenty-five years the structure of the popular music market has remained divided between majors and major independents, who together control about 80 percent of the market, and independents. Takeovers, mergers, and distribution arrangements between various companies have resulted in some relative strengthening and weakening of individual companies, but the relative shares of the market controlled by majors and independents continue to hover around an 80–20 split.[1]

Large corporate labels like CBS bank on million-selling stars to subsidize many of the lesser-known (and riskier) artists. Through personal appearances, product endorsements, commercials, videos, and concert tours the entertainment industry star system is designed to keep the names and faces of major recording artists before the public. This star system is part of the major label's muscular promotional machinery. When combined with an efficient distribution network the result is increased visibility and record sales. With these resources major recording companies maintain a stable of superstar talent and, because they have superior distribution and promotion resources, the proportion of the market share enjoyed by the top labels remains relatively steady. The result is a pattern of market concentration rather than competition. What competition there is really occurs among independents, who operate on the commercial and aesthetic margins of the industry.

With big-name talent on the order of Whitney Houston, Billy Joel, and Bruce Springsteen major labels like CBS or Warner Communications routinely sell records in the hundreds of thousands per unit. In 1982 industry observers estimated (conservatively) the break-even point for major recording firms at between 100,000 and 150,000 sales per record (Sutherland 1982). As the volume of records sold among mega pop stars escalates, large companies routinely aim for gold and platinum records. For stars like Michael Jackson, the standard against which success is judged hovers in the range of a million sales per unit. With such ambitious, but realizable goals, a company is assured of a rapid accumulation of profits once the break-even point of 150,000 units is reached (Frith 1981). For jazz musicians with broad enough popular appeal—Miles Davis, George Benson, Wynton Marsalis, Herbie Hancock, or David Sanborn, for instance—unit sales expectations also reach into the hundreds of thousands.[2]

In the 1980s the aesthetic and commercial success of the surprise hit jazz film "Round Midnight" along with aggressive promotion of jazz superstars by major labels resulted in increased visibility and sales for jazz. This increased visibility and aggressiveness from the recording industry is significant since jazz still accounts for a relatively small share of the total sales of popular music. In 1979 Warner Communications reported that jazz accounted for 4 percent of prerecorded music sales, while rock accounted for 36 percent, soul/R&B/disco 13 percent, country 14 percent, easy listening 14 percent, classical 4 percent, and other music 7 percent (Baskerville 1979: 179; Warner Communications 1980). In a similar study, though using different categories, the Recording Industry Association of America reported that contemporary rock/ pop/soul accounted for 60 percent, country 14 percent, middle of the road 7 percent, jazz 6 percent, classical 6 percent, and "other" 7 percent (Baskerville 1979: 179).

Its relatively small share of the popular music market reflects the fact that jazz is a specialized music whose consumers tend to be more informed about the music and its practitioners than, say, rock and pop consumers. They also follow carefully the careers of major players as well as supporting players. The music does not sell in the same volume as pop and rock records, but the shelf life of jazz recordings is on the average much longer than other popular musics. In terms of the major means of public exposure—radio airplay—jazz recordings seldom enjoy the kind of attention (whether radio or video) that popular music receives. Much less often is there a "jazz hit single" that enjoys repeated radio airplay on tightly for-matted radio and video stations. Jazz radio programmers often work from albums rather than from singles and in more flexible programming formats. Compositions are longer and records move in and out of regular airplay much faster than in tighter Top 10 and Top 20 pop music formats. Although the growing popularity of fusion styles and the commercial success of jazz artists such as Miles Davis, Wynton Marsalis, and Herbie Hancock has led recording companies to apply to jazz promotion and sales strategies ordinarily reserved for pop and rock, audiences are exposed to jazz largely through touring, live concerts, and club appearances.

How is it, then, that small independent record companies survive in the contemporary music business? And, culturally, what is the consequence of their presence? Are these small independent cultural producers (and others such as book pub-lishers, film companies, radio stations) significant repositories and shapers of contemporary American culture? This book explores these issues of cultural production through the ex-periences of Theresa Records. It approaches Theresa's ex-perience as an independent jazz record company in terms of its structural location in the recording industry, especially the way the company manages the various constraints—for ex-ample, distribution—necessary to get its records heard.

Any recording firm, regardless of size, ideology, or or-ganization, must meet basic requirements of production, manufacture, and administration. Production is where the primary aesthetic and artistic requirements are met: songs must be composed, arranged, and recorded; musicians, en-gineers, and other support personnel must be hired and co-ordinated to complete the initial task of recording the music.

Manufacturing is the stage in which the recorded products are transformed into physical artifacts—records, tapes, compact discs, videos—and packaged for presentation to the public. Finally, administration coordinates and manages the various people, resources, and activities so that the company can routinely meet its responsibilities.

At major recording firms the requirements of production, manufacture, and administration are usually met through complex divisions of labor and the organization of the firm into various departments and units. These organizational divisions are primarily bureaucratic. At small independent firms where staffs typically range from one to ten people, such complex and formal arrangements are often inefficient and socially difficult to maintain.

Central to my account of Theresa's story is the members' account—ideology—of their work and their company. Independent cultural production involves more than a simple distinction between big companies and small companies. Therefore, what people at Theresa make of their work and products can help us understand the nature of work, its organization, meaning, and consequence. More importantly, we can address more completely the question of why people persist at this work in an environment that seems to guarantee little except frustration and disappointment.

The modern jazz independent record company's status is derived from a number of elements: the structural location of the company in the popular music industry; reliance on a network of independent record distributors and wholesalers to disseminate and market its products; a set of ideological values that guide the company's aesthetic direction and define its identity and organizational character; and the size of the company and the resources it has available to meet the demands it faces. Collectively these conditions shape the routine operation of a company, influencing its organization, market location, and ideological values (Peterson 1982). Based on the particular combination and expression of these criteria, I have identified three kinds of independent jazz recording firms: structural, mixed, and ideological independents.

Structural independents are distinguished by their search for large commercial markets. For these firms music is primarily a source of financial profits. Production and administration are structured according to bureaucratic forms of social organization and defined by hierarchical decision making. At these companies music tends to be in the stylistic mainstream of the jazz genre. Although these firms have been known to offer innovative musics that push on the stylistic boundaries of the genre—for example, ABC/Impulse! (Giddins 1986)—more often than not their music is predictable and accessible to the widest possible audience. Were it not for limitations of size, scale, and resources, structural independents would for all practical purposes operate like large major corporate recording firms. Except for size, these companies belong in the second tier of major independent firms already mentioned. They include such companies as Concord Jazz and Fantasy Records.

In discussing life at Palo Alto Jazz, Herb Wong, its former president, described the commercial priorities of structural independents:

> Palo Alto was governed . . . by a corporation that had nothing to do with this [music] industry. They were in financial products and services, money market funds, tax free accounts, tax

free funds, . . . federal and state tax refunds, precious metal
funds. What's that got to do with this? The communication
problems about what's important, what's necessary to move
something along was difficult. . . . They decided to go with
the more commercial things and dump the jazz. . .I think
because of that decision they may be doing better financially,
maybe. (Wong 1986)

Wong's description reveals the way in which these companies
are defined by their acceptance of the commercial values and
approaches of the major companies that dominate the popular
music industry. Where they exist, ideological commitments
to jazz, its practitioners, and its tradition are secondary.

Mixed independents are companies that are concerned with
achieving and maintaining commercial success and that operate with ideological commitments to the importance of jazz,
its tradition, and practitioners. While these companies are
certainly in the record business for commercial success, financial rewards are by no means the only objectives that define
them. Like their structural counterparts, these companies
maintain access to the distribution and marketing resources
required to stabilize their economic position and organization,
but musically they also maintain strong commitments to aesthetic vitality and innovation and not just commercial appeal.
BlackHawk, Muse, ECM, and the Italian label Black Saint
strike me as mixed firms.

Different from structural and mixed independents are those
labels where the primary identity and commitment is to maintaining jazz's cultural and aesthetic significance. Although a
requirement for the survival of the labels, the commercial
success of their records (or a search for the elusive hit record)

for many of these companies is a secondary motivation. Many were started by jazz enthusiasts or by musicians to create supportive environments for the music and its practitioners. According to Orrin Keepnews, owner of Landmark Records, love for the music and a desire to be closely involved with the life of jazz motivate these entrepreneurs.

> Alfred Lion and Frank Wolf, Bob Weinstock, . . . myself [Lester] Koeng . . . all began as traditional jazz fans. . . . Also . . . almost without exception, you have the conversion from the fan—from the amateur into the professional. I know I've often said I ruined a perfectly good hobby by getting into this for a living. (Orrin Keepnews 1986); see also George [1985] and Guralnick [1986] for similar accounts about entrepreneur rhythm and blues independents).

This enthusiasm in turn provides these small-scale entrepreneurs with their musical vision and stylistic direction, organizational character, and identity. These ideological commitments are possible because such firms produce very few recordings compared to major firms and they depend on small-scale distribution and promotion. As Keepnews noted, many of these firms do eventually become stable and financially successful enough to provide a living for their owners. Companies such as Theresa Records, Landmark, Contemporary, Bee Hive, India Navigation, and About Time Records are examples of these companies.

Companies with the strongest and most explicit ideological beliefs and most explicit identities tend to be those that are most economically marginal and unstable. Smaller and less burdened with financial and organizational obligations that come with commercial success and large size, many mixed and ideological independents are stylistically adventurous. These firms record some of the most innovative music in jazz. At the same time this innovation and ideological commitment guarantees that these companies will remain economically marginal to majors and structural independents.

Ideological independents are organized on the basis of informal relationships. Here a personal commitment to jazz, its tradition, and its players is central to the daily life of the company. As companies become larger and more commercially successful, they experience greater pressures to protect and maintain their commercial success. There is often less time to consider matters such as the company's public musical identity or stylistic direction. Therefore, the distinction between these various kinds of independents and their commercial success and ideological commitment is an ideal distinction. Indeed, it is not so much a commitment to one set of values or another that governs the behavior of cultural producers as the inefficiency and constraints that must be negotiated to get one's products through various stages of the culture industry. Therefore, the organization, behavior, and values of a cultural organization also reflect adjustment to the environment in which it operates (Ryan and Peterson 1982).

In the case of Theresa Records at least, the primacy of ideological values and aesthetic commitments shifted slightly over time with changes in the company's circumstances and development. As I show in Chapter Three, with Theresa's emergence as a national company came a slow, almost imperceptible shift in the organization and the members' definition of their activity. As the visibility and legitimacy of the company increased, members became more explicitly concerned about increasing record sales, efficient distribution, and effective promotion. They talked often about keeping production costs down and developing a systematic approach to their work. Success also increased the demands on the company's limited resources. Increasingly (and in spite of the ideological values), members were faced with the question of the most effective way to meet these new demands, and, at the same time, maintain commitments to their aesthetic values. While they did not dominate, questions of organizational efficiency, financial solvency, and the commercial appeal of Theresa's music became significant in the day-to-day operation of the company.

The explicit concern of Chapter Four is with the external circumstances and environment in which Theresa operated, especially the independent distribution system and its constraints. This system inevitably shaped the organization of Theresa's work and in the process contributed to Theresa's status as an independent company (Peterson 1982). Together Chapters Three and Four suggest that Theresa Records arrived at its identity as an independent company as a result of the company's management and negotiation of the various external constraints.

Chapter Five explores these external constraints and their impact on Theresa's independent status by shifting the focus to its internal organization and management. Theresa's specific organizational character is also partly the result of the small size of the company, the roots of the social relations of the members in close personal friendship, and the operation of the company out of Kazuko's home. This situation and the ways in which the members identified and defined themselves both contributed to the company's independent status and added to its problems. Theresa's independence was a product of the interaction of these external and internal situations.

The consumption and use of popular culture can be seen as one moment where symbolic struggle occurs between different groups over the definitions, meanings, and practices that organize social life (Gilroy 1987; Hebdige 1979; Willis 1978). Since this struggle also occurs at the point of cultural production, independent cultural organizations such as jazz recording companies, book publishers, newspapers, and radio stations are among the most significant yet ignored sites where important cultural struggles occur. Although the reference is to pop music and not jazz, the following observations by Greg Shaw effectively capture the image of cultural struggle at the level of production:

> We dreamed of putting things back to right, creating the most dynamic pop scene the world has even known and raising it to heights never before reached. We would do it, we thought, by taking the power away from the fat cats and putting it in the hands of the kids. . . . We'd make our own records and as soon as the kids heard the real stuff, they'd drop all that overblown twaddle and pour their bucks into our valiant little cottage industry. Then we'd be self-sufficient and rock an roll would truly belong to the fans for the first time. (Shaw 1982)

"Taking the power away from the fat cats," "the real stuff," "self-sufficiency," and "truly belong to the fans," all ideologically express, quite literally, ways of producing culture for the companies that I am concerned about. In commercially dominated popular music industry the small ideological independent recording company is an environment where there creation and dissemination of the "real stuff" can and does routinely occur. In contrast to the dominance of commercial values and the attendant social organization that defines and organizes the conditions of production in order to maximize profits and maintain efficiency, these small companies represent another way of creating culture. It is in the meanings, organization, and experiences involved in the production of cultural products that alternative representations and expressions are possible—alternative, that is, to the products and processes that emanate from the dominant commercial and bureaucratic sectors of the culture industry. This image of cultural struggle, then, includes the processes of production, the products that are created, and the experiences, traditions, and meanings for creators and users that these experiences represent. In this case the real stuff is not merely or primarily music created for the commercial market but music that expresses the life ways, experiences, and visions of its practioners and the communities/traditions to which they belong.

The experiences of Theresa Records suggests that it is possible to organize cultural production according to an aesthetic vision. This, of course, comes at considerable cost. Theresa's case shows how independent record companies routinely create different, innovative, occasionally alternative cultural forms. Firms like Theresa are not unique in this respect since "the real stuff" and alternative forms sometimes come from the quarters of large, corporately run firms (Frith 1981; Gitlin 1982). The point is that, clearly in the case of jazz, the cultural significance of a small firm like Theresa is far out of proportion to its size, profits, or share of the industry (Keepnews 1979).

The notion of cultural struggle also refers to the considerable control that musicians and company members exercise over their work and their products. At Theresa this control was expressed as the commitment to musician's musical judgments, the primacy of aesthetic rather than commercial values, and the use of personal and collaborative social organization. In the broader environment of the commercial music industry these expressions are rare or in some tension with commercial and bureaucratic values.

Many small independent recording companies fail because of business and organizational incompetence. Such incompetence notwithstanding, a significant number of failures also result from the broader structural environment of the popular music industry, where problems of distribution, cash flow, limited resources, and a ceaseless drive for profits present major impediments. Nevertheless, whether control of production is expressed in aesthetic, political, or economic terms, the experiences of independents represent a specific approach to producing culture.

The flip side to this potential for alternative cultural production and the exercise of social control are the social constraints faced by small ideological independent producers. Although the threshold required for the financial solvency of the small independent is much lower than that for major corporate companies, independents, regardless of their aesthetic position and mode of organization, must still distribute, promote, and sell their records. They must also attract and cultivate new audiences and they must do so in an environment where larger companies have a significant advantage over the control of economic and organizational resources. We will see in Chapter Five, small size and informally based social relations, which were assets of Theresa, at the same time presented serious impediments to the organizational stability and financial control required to survive in the record business.

The experiences of Theresa Records (and to a lesser extent BlackHawk and Landmark Records) indicate just how various independent jazz recording firms respond to these conflicting demands and requirements. At Theresa, Allen and Kazuko grappled with ideological challenges to their aesthetic commitments, the stability of their operation, and the financial need to make more commercially appealing music. Theresa's story suggests that the constraints faced by independent companies led to constant organizational and ideological adjustment in all aspects of the operation. Various members of Theresa's staff were let go and regular debates about the release of commercial material (as opposed to the music to which members were committed) became more frequent, and the number of records released decreased as the force of the constraints became more powerful. These and other adjustments reveal the limits of independent cultural production in the modern commercial music business.[3]

Since independent firms do not exist in isolation from the political and economic organization of the modern music industry a somewhat more functional view of the significance of independent firms than the idea of cultural struggle should at least be mentioned. In this view small jazz independents function very much like professional sports farm teams, providing larger and wealthier organizations like major record companies with potential music and artists. This particular division of labor occurs because of differences in firms and their location in the recording industry. The smaller independents can take greater aesthetic and financial risks than majors and can therefore more effectively scout, introduce, and develop new artists. Once new talent is tested in the marketplace, the major companies, with their superior distribution and promotional resources, can further develop the careers of these artists. In this view, the distinction between independents and majors is one of degree rather than kind.

In this functionalist view, the relationship between the major recording companies and the smaller independents is not at all antagonistic since it is an expression of the economic structure and division of labor in the music industry. Indeed, the small independent's role is to keep the industry majors supplied with fresh, groomed, and tested talent. Where small independents have historically taken the lead in the documentation and dissemination of stylistically marginal, innovative, and noncommercial music such as blues, jazz, and gospel, they have very often operated according to the same exploitative and racist practices as their larger and more powerful counterparts (Dixon and Goodrich 1970; Foreman 1968; Frith 1981).

Both the functionalist reading and the idea that small jazz independents are sites of cultural struggle have some merit. That is to say, the small jazz independent has the possibility for presenting some of the most vital and progressive expressions in the jazz tradition. Yet because of its structural location in the popular music business—with its division of labor, segmentation, and economic and organizational constraints— the jazz independent must constantly negotiate the constraints required to remain in business, effectively managing the requirements of distribution, promotion, and sales. On top of this, the musicians with whom it works and the products it creates are always fair game for absorption by larger, more resourceful companies.

If these readings of the independent are partially correct, then how should we assess the more general impact and status of the independent recording firm in the broader popular music industry? In the final chapter, I suggest that the significance of Theresa Records as a contemporary cultural producer is not limited to or measured by the number of records it sells, the share of jazz sales it controls, or the level of profits it generates. In fact, the economic significance of this company is, at best, negligible (Chapple and Garofalo 1977; Frith 1981; Denisoff 1975). Aesthetically and culturally, however, the significance of companies like Theresa rests with their existence as vehicles for the presentation and documentation of music that continues to fuel the jazz tradition.

These small companies, at least in the case of jazz, are the major outlets for music that enjoy limited commercial exposure in the recording industry as it is now constituted. These firms are also the primary means of introducing new and innovative music to the industry and the public. Through their musicians and music, these companies exert pressure on the aesthetic and stylistic boundaries of the otherwise conservative popular and jazz music industries. Precisely because Theresa operates according to aesthetic values shared by owners and musicians, it serves as a limited vehicle through which symbolic challenges to dominant cultural and aesthetic patterns are expressed.

T W O

INDEPENDENTS AND THE AMERICAN MUSIC INDUSTRY

I think the majors are great for big business but I never thought of music as big business. By our nature as independents I think we care more for the music we present. We don't have to be victims of volume. We have the spirit to test our instincts constantly. I'm sure we're all in the right line of work.

Stan Marshall 1980

Stan Marshall identifies some rather fundamental differences between independent and major recording firms. Perhaps the most significant difference is the primacy of business and music for independents and majors. Is this an artificial distinction? Do independents care more about music rather than about profits and does the distinction between independents and majors also imply a tension between commerce and aesthetics in the popular music industry? This chapter examines these issues by locating the independent record company in the broader social history of the popular music industry. I also describe, more precisely, the conception of the independent recording firm in terms of the ideologies, values, and characteristics that define its activity rather than only in terms of structural factors such as size, sales, and market shares.

Through their control over production and distribution large major companies exercise considerable influence over the choices of music available to be public. Major media and cultural organizations routinely create, appropriate, absorb, and deflect alternatives to the commercially dominant music they produce. To maintain their relative shares of the popular markets, major companies must remain sensitive to the shifts in practices and taste that regularly occur in the turbulent popular music market. Musically this means that obsolescence is structured into the process of making music (Baskerville 1979; Chapple and Garofalo 1977; Frith 1981; Peterson and Berger 1975). Market domination by major companies is sustained in several ways: through control of the stylistic boundaries, through bureaucratic organization, through control of the major mechanisms of dissemination and exposure, and through superior resources—access to producers, artists, and gatekeepers who organize the production and presentation of popular music.

Large major companies, for example, daily receive hundreds of songs, tapes, and other unsolicited materials submitted by musicians in search of recording and performance outlets (Hirsch 1969). The majority of these submissions never reach the inner circles of these companies because of financial, organizational, and taste demands that guide the identification and selection process.[1] These constraints keep major companies focused on music that appeals to the widest possible audience (Denisoff 1975; Frith 1981). At every stage of production, gatekeepers operate in accord with various organizational, professional, and aesthetic criteria to filter and shape ideas that enter the company (Hirsch 1969, 1972; Kealy 1982; Ryan and Peterson 1982).[2] A consequence of this selection process is the subordination of the artists and the cultural artifact to the organizational and financial priorities of the processing organization (Becker 1982).

Many members of the music business argue that this structure and process is the most efficient way to organize their work given the inherent turbulence of the market. These organizational and financial priorities help to sustain the monopoly of major companies. In this environment, too many stylistic risks can easily result in financial disasters. As a result, popular styles are milked for maximum exposure. In the process, the stylistic choices available to consumers are preselected and therefore limited (Garofalo 1987).

In the long run, organizational, stylistic, and market priorities force major record companies to operate at levels guaranteed to generate profits (Hirsch 1978). For specific forms and styles of music such as those with limited commercial appeal, this often means that either they are made to conform to the requirements necessary for commercial success or they remain marginal until there is sufficient demand to warrant investments by major companies. The economic pressures and organizational logic of major companies result in limitations on the range of musical choices within the cultural mainstream.

Major companies operate most effectively when they are able to respond to clearly established and organized markets (Denisoff 1975; Frith 1981; Peterson and Berger 1975). Major companies do occasionally produce stylistically innovative and different music. By and large, however, innovative musics originate from outside major companies. They typically come from small independents located on the margins of the music industry.

> The music business is organized around the realities of overproduction—its daily practices reflect not the problems of creating needs, but responding to them. Few labels have the capital or the courage to risk stirring up new demands, and the record industry has always made its money by picking up on needs independently expressed: punk rock for example was developed as a musical style by musicians and audiences operating outside of the usual record business relationships; it was then taken over and exploited by record companies only when its market potential seemed assured. (Frith 1981: 62)

By definition, small independent cultural producers do not control large shares of the popular music market and some are amateurish, inefficient, and run by romantic enthusiasts whose management strategies come from small cottage industries. Yet, as Frith observes, these companies are sites of some of the most innovative and vibrant activity in the modern culture industry. Independent recording companies have a formidable place in the development of American popular music (George 1985; Guralnick 1986). Although they have a history of high mortality, independents continue to emerge and persist in the face of increasing corporate concentration, growing competition from other forms of entertainment and leisure, limited markets, and often inefficient distribution. Because these small companies are the source of much that is creative and lasting in American popular music, accounts of the evolution of popular music must include attention to their participation and significance. Their influence on the aesthetic fabric of American culture far exceeds their size, power, and economic success.

The greatest proliferation of the independent record company in American popular music occurred during two major periods: from 1947 to 1957 and from 1967 to 1977 (Chapple and Garofalo 1977; Peterson and Berger 1975). Their rise is related to specific transformations in the structure of the popular music industry. Periods of greatest activity by independents also correspond to some extent to the introduction of significant musical innovations. For instance, in the 1920s and 1930s the conservatism of Tin Pan Alley was vitalized and permanently altered by African American–based blues and popular music. Although in the 1940s the most visible and popular musics of the period were dominated by media-appointed white heroes, their musical dominance was eventually challenged by the growing popularity of rhythm and blues, bebop, and country western forms. In both periods, independent recording companies provided outlets for the new music and its artists (Berger 1947; Leonard 1962).

In the 1950s small independent recording companies, radio stations, promotion networks, and performance venues were central to the emergence of the new jazz (bebop), country, and rhythm and blues (Ryan 1985). The coalescence of these elements of the recording and broadcasting industry were a part of a larger challenge to the dominance of middle-class sensibilities and organizations. The Broadcast Music Association (BMI), a licensing organization, was formed in the 1940s as an alternative to the powerful American Society of Composers, Artists and Publishers (ASCAP) (Garofalo and Chapple 1980; Ryan 1985). BMI opposed the fee structure of ASCAP and together with radio stations and the new generation of artists and their independent recording firms challenged the hegemony of ASCAP by presenting the musics of rural southern blacks, poor whites, and other groups routinely excluded from the narrow New York–Hollywood network of show tunes, movie sound tracks, big band swing, and Tin Pan Alley songs.

By the 1960s the stylistic dominance of easy listening music performed by popular middle-of-the-road male crooners like Frank Sinatra, Bing Crosby, and Pat Boone was seriously eroded by rock and roll. Organizationally this challenge came from independents and had musical roots in jazz and rhythm and blues from the previous decade, white-based rock a' billy, and the blues-inspired invasion of English rock led by the Beatles and the Rolling Stones (Chapple and Garofalo 1977; Frith 1981; Guralnick 1986).

In jazz, the relationship between majors and independents, stylistic innovation and aesthetic dominance, has lacked this high drama. Beginning in the 1940s and continuing into the late 1960s the major recording life and vitality of jazz, except in the case of major "stars," remained essentially uncontested and in the hands of small and medium-sized independent recording firms. Consequently, the history of the jazz independents and their impact on the general popular music industry is the story of the tenacity and survival of companies like Blue Note, Savoy, Riverside, Prestige, Fantasy (in its formative periods), and Contemporary. The history of these firms, especially their operation, ideologies, and relationships to the existing musics and recording companies of their day, anticipated and shaped the contemporary experiences of Theresa Records and others like it.

With the disappearance of many independent companies active in the 1950s and 1960s has come the increasing involvement in jazz of major recording companies like Columbia Records and Warner Brothers. This involvement has coincided with the popularization and commercialization of fusion as a subgenre in jazz; with its broad commercial appeal, it is musically more accessible to the general public and for larger companies easier to promote. In spite of this increased participation in jazz by majors, new independent recording firms continue to appear.

In the 1980s the pattern of stylistic innovation from independents and absorption by majors continues. Reggae, disco, punk, and rap musics, for instance, each began in obscurity but now enjoy mainstream commercial acceptance (George 1982; Hebdige 1979; Toop 1984). In each case these powerful bursts of stylistic innovation were introduced by independents. Their introduction also resulted in dramatic shifts in the organization and presentation of popular music. These shifts have been musical: in the case of rap, the introduction of scratching and rap; in the case of reggae, the introduction of the back beat and the heavy rhythmic emphasis. The shifts have also been structural. Along with the stylistic "freshness" of disco, rap, and punk came new methods of distribution, promotion, and marketing. Rap music and disco developed through a series of underground networks, house parties, and dance venues (Toop 1984). Under these conditions new music could be easily previewed, exchanged, and introduced to audiences by disc jockeys without negotiating the formal promotion or distribution channels of the music industry.

Large major companies got involved and quickly organized these alternative and parallel networks by sponsoring and financing disc jockey pools, supplying them with their own releases, and signing rap performers to lucrative contracts (Frith 1981; Toop 1984). These parallel networks have now been incorporated into the distribution and promotional approaches of major companies.

The Concept of Independence

I have been making the case that the experience and approach to making records outside the major companies is important American musical history. However, even in this context independent recording companies have not been immune to transformations in the recording industry. Rather, the distinction between independents and majors, big and small companies, needs greater specification. By offering this clarification, I want to recover the notion of independent cultural production from the overeconomistic and structural meanings it has come to have.

Economic and organizational changes in the music industry since the 1940s have slowly eroded the idea of the independent recording firm. "Today there is almost no such thing as an independent label. . . . When we speak of an independent label what is usually meant is that a firm, large or small, is dependent on another company to handle its distribution" (Baskerville 1979: 307). While, in general, this description is correct, it seems to me to be limited and at best meaningful only in relationship to major companies. It fails to appreciate the value and potential that these small firms represent for the creation and presentation of different cultural forms. In the specific case of jazz the notion of independent recording firms is still useful and indeed requires conceptual expansion. Significant to a firm's structural location and methods of distribution are its ideological definitions, aesthetic commitments, and organizational character. These nonstructural characteristics account for the uniqueness of the independent, especially the jazz independent.

The popular conception of the independent record company runs counter to our intuitive understanding. In the recording business, the concept of independence, as Baskerville observed, really suggests dependence more than the freedom or control that might be attributed to the term. Historically, "independence" describes an economic and organizational relationship between a record company and an (independent) distributor in which the latter assumes primary responsibility for the dissemination, promotion, and sale of the former's records. Administrative and financial control of the distributor remains outside the recording company, and the relationship between the label and the distributor is interdependent. While the distributor works in the interest of the record company, the distributor is directly influenced by constraints different from those faced by the recording firm.

The independent distribution system operates like this: The independent record company sells its products to a network of independent distributors, which in turn sells the records to a network of record retailers and related businesses. These retailers then resell the records to the public. In this arrangement, the independent distributor functions as a wholesaler, buying products from the record label and selling them to the retailer. Often this system of independent distribution works against small firms, whose records may be specialized, unpopular, or slow to sell. All records, no matter what their sales pattern, initially require the time and attention of company personnel and distributors to bring them to the attention of the public and the various gatekeepers. The process is especially relevant to jazz records, which are traditionally slow sellers.

Selling records in this fashion does not particularly help the economic survival of the independent distributor. It is simply too demanding and time-consuming for the economic returns it produces. As a result, most slow-moving records—even though they promise steady sales—are either ignored or not pushed very aggressively, not because they are bad records but because they tie up the distribution system.

A key to the distributor's success is a record's popularity, since retailers are interested mainly in records that move quickly and easily, regardless of their stylistic importance or aesthetic significance. It is in the best interest of the independent record distributor to carry several different labels, especially those with proven and consistent products. The independent distribution system is built on the logic of proven success and consistency.

Given this system, the distinction between majors and independents was most relevant in the 1950s, when the scale of operation, vertical integration, musical diversity, catalogue size, and a large and diverse artist roster characterized a few companies in the popular music industry. Until the mid-1960s most if not all the companies in the music industry used some form of independent record distribution. During this period the (independent) distributor was such a crucial link in the manufacturing process that records were very often designed and packaged with the distributor or "record seller" rather than the public in mind (Frith 1981; Ryan and Peterson 1982).

This system of record distribution dominated the popular music industry until large major companies extended their ownership and control to manufacturing, distribution, and retail. By this point, however, these explicit structural distinctions had become blurred. The definition of "'majors' broadened to include companies that were selling as many records as the old majors but that, nevertheless, did not do their own pressing and often used independent distributors" (Chapple and Garofalo, 1977: 15). This extension of control eliminated the reliance of major companies on the independent distributor because it was less expensive and more efficient and ensured greater control and accountability.[3]

Since smaller, less resourceful companies continue to depend on this system, is it fair to say that they are simply smaller versions of the larger companies? The central theme of this book is that they are not and that the lack of control over distribution only described one aspect of the independent experience. Independent recording firms operate with a distinctive set of meanings, relationships, and approaches to cultural production.

The Big versus Small Debate in Popular Music

With their proverbial ears to the ground, independent firms were and remain in the best position to identify and respond to innovation and diversity (Peterson and Berger 1975; Rothenbuhler and Dimmick 1982). Once these innovative musics and aesthetic possibilities are identified, then major companies enter (or re-enter) a specific market and with their superior marketing, promotion, and distribution resource establish control.

In their study of post-World War II changes in the composition of the American popular music industry, sociologists Richard Peterson and David Berger examined the relationship between majors and independents and its impact on musical diversity. They discovered an inverse relationship between the degree of monopoly control by major companies (characterized by the dominance in sales of a few large firms) and the range of musical diversity available to popular music consumers (Peterson and Berger 1975). Alternating with long stretches of monopolistic control were short periods of musical diversity. The periods of stylistic diversity were defined by a highly competitive market where a large number of independent firms were responsible for top-selling records. Periods of monopoly control were distinguished by stylistic homogeneity while the short periods of competition were defined stylistically by diversity and innovation.

British music critic and sociologist Simon Frith took issue with this view of the relationship between majors and independents and their impact on musical development, because it fails to appreciate that all firms in the popular music industry, regardless of size or location, are there to maximize profits (Frith 1981). With regard to politics or music, it matters little whether a firm is large or small, independent or major (Frith 1981; Garofalo 1987). Moreover, the account by Peterson and Berger minimizes the role of the consumer, who has considerably more influence (albeit indirectly) in matters of musical choice, use, and diversity (Frith 1986).

The sharp distinction between large and small companies presents other difficulties as well. It confuses what is essentially a structural division of labor and organizational response by the music industry to its lack of control over the market and popular tastes (Frith 1981). The alternating cycles of con-

trol and competition (and the musical diversity and homogeneity that accompany them) express the constant adjustment
by large major companies to markets they cannot completely
control. As audiences and their social configurations change,
large firms cautiously follow the shifts, since they cannot lead
or anticipate them (Denisoff 1975). As a result of the uncertainty created by these constant shifts, large firms must continually identify, refine, and extend the locus of their control
in the areas of production, distribution, and consumption
(Garofalo 1987). This is not so much a cyclical process as a
groping toward a more permanent condition of control. Independents do not face this problem so dramatically since
they are very often the first ones to register changes and
developments.

Firth's rejection of the implicit opposition between independents and majors rests on two additional points. The separation leads to an almost romantic regard for small
entrepreneurs and owners, as if their stakes and involvement
in the music business were somehow more noble than those
of the majors. Such romantic notions do not hold up since
some of the most blatant exploitation of musicians, especially
black musicians, has come at the hands of independent recording entrepreneurs. The polarization of large and small
firms also places musics produced by these firms on a con-
tinuum ranging from commercial and corrupt music produced by majors on one end to authentic independent music
on the other.

I share Firth's general skepticism about the uncritical celebration of independents and the blanket condemnation of
majors. Nevertheless, certain political values and aesthetic
challenges to the dominant commercial music manufactured

by major companies do find expression among independent firms (e.g., punk and rap musics). More importantly, where these independent pulses do find expression they are not simply differences in intensity (from majors). The aesthetic and economic patterns identified by Peterson and Berger have, in fact, become a permanent and systematic division of labor in the popular music industry (Garofalo 1987).

The reorganization of the American popular music industry since the 1960s, including the introduction of new technologies and the ability of major companies to influence government regulation of the recording industry, means that major companies no longer need to absorb the higher costs and risks required to monitor and adjust to subtle shifts in the market.

Major recording firms are economically and organizationally powerful precisely because they have the financial resources to monopolize and control all phases of the production and distribution process while independents do not.[4] Uncertainty in the marketplace for majors is not a simple matter of aesthetic choice but a calculated gamble based on the proportion of a given market that a company controls. In those cases where firms control a significant portion of the market, the issue is not so much deciding what particular music to release as specifying the economic terms within which a given set of financial investments (e.g., talent, studio time, promotion) will generate a given level of financial return. Major firms in the contemporary American recording industry might be regarded as banks more than as recording companies since what they do is to invest, finance, and administer various aspects of the production, distribution, and promotion process.

The size or scale of a company, its musical diversity, catalogue size, degree of structural integration in the production
process, are all structural indicators of whether or not a firm
is a major or independent.

> The product lines of major labels tend to span the entire gamut
> of music from classical to jazz, rock, country and all other
> forms. The major labels tend to be integrated vertically own-
> ing their own studios, pressing plants, and distribution facil-
> ities. In contrast, independents tend to concentrate on one
> particular category of music such as jazz and seldom produce
> records outside of the range of their main interest. (Connelly
> 1981: 2)

The need for this division of labor in the first place and
the need for continuous market and stylistic adjustment by
majors suggest that their control is incomplete. In this new
and permanent division of labor, aesthetic risks are taken by
small independents without the economic consequences that
large companies run. Once markets have been identified, tastes
registered, and talent groomed by the small companies, the
majors simply buy out an artist's contract and promote and
distribute that artist on a larger scale. The very institution-
alization of the structure of the contemporary industrial system of music making is evidence that major companies do
exercise specific, but not necessarily complete, control (Garofalo 1987).

In relationship to major companies and their structural
characteristics, the notion of "independent" captures only one
dimension of the small record company's experience (Baskerville 1979; Frith 1981). It is certainly true that firms like

Theresa Records are shaped (and often battered) by the complex structural contingencies (distribution, scale of operation) that impinge on them. Their independent status is also a product of the ideologies, organization, and meanings that the members construct for themselves, their music, their audiences, and their artists.

The significance of these aesthetic, political, and ideological differences among various kinds of firms is potentially lost in the collapse of majors/independents or big/little firms. Also lost are activities and developments that occur in the cracks and spaces of social and cultural life where majors do not venture. While I also have some reservations about making too much of the distinctions between independents and majors, I do want to give resonance to the voices and experiences of people who choose to perform and work in the context of the small independent recording company.

Theresa's experience suggests that independent labels are not just smaller versions of Columbia Records, but that they represent a different sensibility in making records. They reflect marginal and innovative social and cultural experiences.

THREE

THE RISE OF THERESA
RECORDS

Distributors and others in the business gave us high and made it known that we would be taken seriously as an important jazz label.

Allen

In Theresa's early years, its musical focus was exclusively on San Francisco Bay area musicians. Between 1975 and 1980 the company released records by these musicians, secured distribution deals, and presented its artists in local concert and club appearances. Allen drew heavily on a network of musicians who were regular members of various performance units in the area for early material released by Theresa. These musicians included saxophonist Bishop Norman Williams, bassist James Leary, arranger and bandleader David Hardiman, pianist Ed Kelly, and percussionist Babatunde.

For example, Bishop Norman Williams', working band, the One Mind Experience, was as journalist Blair Jackson describes, the musical basis for Theresa's first record:

They [the Bishop Norman Williams Band] gigged steadily at the now defunct scene on upper Filmore and gained a considerable following throughout the city. . . . A record seemed to be the logical next step for the group, so they went into a

> local studio and made a demo which they showed to various
> labels. . . . (Jackson 1979; p. 10)

The band initially sought a recording contract with CBS and
Fantasy Records. Allen eventually took the tapes to Arhoolee
and Blue Note Records. "Blue Note came the closest to signing the band, but in the end there were no firm offers. And
that's when Allen . . . became a record company. The resulting album, *The Bishop* was out as the first release on
[Allen's] Theresa Record label" (Jackson 1979).

    The Bishop featured the work of Williams, a disciple of
Charlie Parker, whose musical origins are modern bebop.[1]
Among the musicians who appeared on *The Bishop* were a
core of colleagues and friends who became central players
during Theresa's formative years: Williams on alto, Paul at
the piano, Allen on trumpet. *The Bishop*'s selections were
largely derivative and acknowledged the musical influences
of the period. Uneven and eclectic in approach, the music,
nevertheless, swings.

    Side one opened with a straight-ahead kicker called "Figure
Eight." The remaining three compositions were by Paul.
"Don't Go 'Way" was distinguished by a latin rhythmic pat-
tern and features Williams on a short but searing alto solo.
This was followed by the more subdued, but no less effective
"Christina." The second side opened with a composition that
reflected the varied electronic influences of the early seventies.
At their best these experimentations, led by Herbie Hancock
and Miles Davis, combined the rhythm and electronic sounds
of rock with the improvisational and harmonic approaches
of jazz. Other selections included a homage to John Coltrane
("Trane's Paradise," a reference to Coltrane's "Niama") and

the final selection, "Ole' Brown," which typified the music of the period but included interesting references to Ornette Coleman's innovative saxophone style.

This initial record established the basic stylistic directions for Allen and members of the company to sharpen through the years; producing it taught them some valuable lessons about the workings of the recording business. Other independent companies such as Arhoolee Records and Rounder Records offered Allen important advice on the operation of the music business as well as significant distribution support. Not surprisingly Theresa did not make any money on this record; in fact it lost some of its records through its inexperience with independent distributors. These hard lessons notwithstanding, by the release of the next record, *Bishop's Bag* (TR102), Allen confessed to having been bitten by the record bug: "I got sucked into it at that time and decided to make the record with Ed Kelly . . . [TR103]" (Allen 1986).

In 1976, the recording industry climate for small independent firms was generally favorable, and Allen believed that conditions would at the very least allow him to make a reasonable return on his financial investment. As a working musician and friend of many musicians in the area Allen felt a personal commitment to developing a recording company sensitive to the musician's viewpoint.

In its early months Theresa fully experienced the considerable industry pressures exerted on small independents. Rising production costs and distribution problems were the most troublesome. Allen remembered this as a period of learning from mistakes about the operation of the record business, especially in distribution and promotion: "I didn't know where to send records. I was relying on distributors to get the records out. They had people on their staffs. . . . I realized later that radio stations had to get records. . . . By the double album [TR108/109] I got the radio stations and that boosted my morale" (Allen 1986).

From 1976 to 1980 Theresa's contact with the essential components of the record business (distribution, promotion, and radio airplay) was limited to the San Francisco Bay area and urban areas in the East and the Midwest. Theresa's distribution strategy was to send records into a few key markets where its artists were likely to be known or where a jazz audience was already established.

Initially distributors were apprehensive about handling Theresa's records because the company was small and new, with neither an established reputation nor a clear direction. Lacking regularized distribution relationships, Theresa confronted the circular problems characteristic of start-up operations—cash flow and the lack of consistent exposure for its artists and records. Allen recalled:

> Getting independent distributors interested in the first place is difficult. Getting paid by them is next to impossible. Unless you want to spend your time trying to collect from distributors, you're going to be ignored when you ask for payment. You usually end up spending more time writing letters trying to get a few dollars than its worth. (Jackson 1979: 10)

Kazuko also had similar recollections: "Distributors will pay you on the basis of how well your records are selling. . . . There were a lot of distributors who just didn't acknowledge our existence; they took our product but they didn't return any, they didn't pay anything." (Kazuko 1981). This response by distributors continued to frustrate Theresa's efforts to develop exposure outside of the Bay area, and in turn to generate sales. Distributors, Allen observed, wanted to know that Theresa would be around, that it would continue to put out records, and, most importantly, that money could be made in the process.

> You know when you're dealing with these distributors, there's maybe a third of them that you're worried about that you're never gonna get paid. . . . And see when this recession in records kinda came about . . ., I'd say about two years ago when it really hit, the majors stopped buying, they cut way back on everything. What they [the distributors] bought mostly were big sellers and big company labels. Small record companies suffered a lot more proportionally. In other words, somebody might have ordered fifty records and only put five or ten in the store; so they're not in the store and so people go out and look for them in the store and usually they forget about it. (Allen 1981)

With little ability to persuade distributors to take a chance on them Allen and Kazuko relied on heavily on family, friends, musicians, and members of the company to help with distribution and promotion. Everyone associated with the company sold and talked up Theresa's records. It was common, for example, to see stacks of records for sale at concerts and club appearances by the One Mind Experience. This approach to resolving their distribution problems actually served the company well in the long run. First, this very personal nature of promoting records and selling the company actively involved all the members, giving them a greater personal investment in the company. Second, the strategy helped to maximize Theresa's limited resources. The direct involvement of musicians and various support personnel also became the social basis of Theresa's organization in which core members had personal as well as professional stakes in the company's success.

Another response to their distribution problems was to alter the musical focus of the company. Allen and Kazuko soon realized that a core of recognizable artists with a proven track record could help the company achieve financial stability and a public reputation. The next four albums released by Theresa included nationally recognized musicians.

Theresa's response to its distribution situation is not unusual for small cultural organizations with limited power and resources; cultural products are as much organized to meet the requirements of processing and distribution organizations as those of the audience. This was evident from Theresa's next three releases (Becker 1982; Ryan and Peterson 1982; Ryan 1985):

> Theresa next put out "Bishop's Bag" which won the Bay Area Music Award for the best jazz album . . . for Williams and Theresa. Pianist Ed Kelly's beautiful "Music from the Black Museum" and a stunning album of contemporary big band tunes by David Hardiman and the San Francisco Big Band. This apparent show of strength by Theresa coupled by the appearance of nationally known reedman David Liebman on Bishop's record led to a dramatically increased distribution network for the label (particularly in the east), more airplay and not surprisingly more records sold." (Jackson 1979: 10)

Released in 1978, *Bishop's Bag* (TR102) featured Bishop Norman Williams and guest tenor saxophonist David Liebman on several tunes. Liebman appeared in various combinations with Williams, Hadley Caliman on saxophones, Allen and Mark Isham on trumpets, Babatunde on congas, Mike Howell on guitar, and Paul at the piano. Mike Clark and Curtis Ohlson completed the personnel on drums and bass.

Owing to its large ensemble, the record had a fuller and brighter sound than the previous Williams record (TR101). The opening side featured two rather long tunes, one by Paul and one by Williams. "Hip Funk" was very much a song in search of its identity: part funk with a lazy but insistent groove over which an equally reserved but complex melodic line was played by the full ensemble. Electronic effects and percussive accents provided occasional color and punctuation. Paul's "One Mind Experience" played by a small ensemble suggested the fusion influences of the period.

The second side of the album was more consistently satisfying. In execution and composition "For Lee," Williams' dedication to trumpeter Lee Morgan, with its hard bop melodic and rhythmic structure, was the most interesting song on the record. Smaller units played "Billy Ballet," which had a decidedly latin temperament and rhythmic approach, and "Dolphy." Liebman was at his best on "Dolphy"; adding to the fullness of the quintet with a lean sound and agile approach to the horn, he moved through the lines of the tune with ease and excitement. Williams provided an effective contrast to Liebman's solo with work in the upper registers of the alto.

With its range of themes and artists, this record was important for Theresa's emerging public identity and reputation as a record company. By now there was little doubt that Allen was serious about Theresa and that he intended to remain in the music business. Where *The Bishop* helped launch the label and get its musicians before the public, *Bishop's Bag* effectively got the attention of both the music industry and the public.

In 1978 also came a beautifully conceived if not fully realized project featuring pianist/composer Ed Kelly. Kelly, who would eventually play a key role in bringing Pharoah Sanders to Theresa, was a fixture in the Bay area, especially the East Bay. *Music from the Black Museum* (TR103), with Kelly at the piano, Smiley Winters on drums, and Peter Barshay on bass with Willie Reeves on conga, included a Kelly original and materials by other composers. Rather than a display of his compositional skills, TR103 served as a performance vehicle for Kelly and his colleagues. It was an effective display of shifting moods, textures, and styles. Kelly's command and ease of playing, along with the band's collective energy, compensated for the record's lack of interesting material. Notably, the one Kelly original anticipated in mood and feeling directions that Pharoah would later bring to the company. Although it did not make a big splash outside the Bay area, TR103 was important because it was an early indication of Theresa's maturing musical directions.

It'll Be All Right by David Hardiman and the San Francisco All Star Big Band was the fourth record released by Theresa (TR104); this record also featured Bay area musicians. Under the name the San Francisco All Star Big Band, Hardiman assembled some of the most important players in the area. According to Allen the band was formed in September 1975 under the auspices of the San Francisco Arts Commission Neighborhood Arts Program (liner notes, TR104, 1978). Material on the album ranged from jazz and blues standards like Coltrane's "Giant Steps" and Percy Mayfield's "Please Send Me Someone to Love" to pop and show tunes such as "Time

After Time" by Stein Cohen. The sound of the record was bright and full. (In the record liner notes one reviewer described the band as having a "solid, Basie style foundation with plenty of space and freedom for improvisation [liner notes, TR104].) For only the fourth record of a young record company, the date was a musical success. But the financial picture of the company at this point was another matter.

Allen initially financed Theresa from personal resources; Kazuko was initially an enthusiastic supporter who became Allen's full-time partner through her interest and financial investments in the company. Both were driven by a passion for jazz and the idea that they could make it financially in the record business. As time went on, their commitment to the music and musicians as well as their financial investments grew. By the time the fourth record was made, additional financial resources were necessary to complete projects to which they were already committed. To clear away existing commitments and to finance new projects, Allen took out a couple of second mortgages on homes he owned jointly with his former wife. Capital from the second mortgage along with investments from Kazuko became the basis for the financial life of the company through its first four years. Subsequent projects were financed by the profits from a formula that Allen patented and sold through his research as a polymer chemist. This financial latitude was especially important in this period of Theresa's greatest growth and development as a record company; during this period the company hired additional office personnel, completed existing projects, started significant recording projects with Pharoah, and eventually moved out of Kazuko's home to an office in Albany, California. Most significantly, profits from the sale of Allen's patents enabled him to secure an early retirement from his career as a research scientist and devote his energies full time to the record company.

Beyond the Bay Area: Theresa as a National Company

The growth of Theresa Records from a small, obscure regional independent to a nationally recognized company occurred in the years between 1980 and 1983. This movement was related to two important developments whose origins lie in the period between 1978 and 1980.

The release of TR102, which featured reedman Liebman, was a small but significant step toward establishing Theresa's credibility with its distributors and its growing audience. With the release of TR104 Allen (1981) "realized" as he put it, "that we couldn't sell just local people." Thus on TR105, following the pattern established by the appearance of Liebman on TR102, appeared respected baritone saxophonist Pepper Adams. Adams agumented a Bishop Norman Williams unit that now included Allen, Paul, and Babatunde as principal members with trumpeter Warren Gale, drummer Larry Hancock, Curtis Ohlson on bass, Marvin Williams on tenor, and Mark Isham on synthesizer. The release of TR105—*One for Bird*—and TR106—*Ed Kelly and Friend*—in many respects reinforced Theresa's growing reputation as a small but significant firm in the jazz recording business.

Issued in 1979, *One for Bird* (TR105) was the last collaboration on record between Theresa and Bishop Norman Williams. The collaboration ended, not because of aesthetic differences, but because Allen felt pressures to include national artists as a strategy to promote Theresa's records. According to Allen, Bishop Norman Williams and Ed Kelly also wanted to stay close to their various responsibilities and relationships in the Bay area rather than tour.

One for Bird retained the same instrumental and stylistic allegiances to modern bebop as Williams' previous Theresa releases. If *Bishop's Bag* was the most intense and passionate of the three Williams sessions on Theresa, *One for Bird* was the most focused and best conceived. All the elements—editing, pacing, personnel, song placement and selection, recording quality, spirit, packaging—that go into making a successful record came together on TR105.

The Williams original "Tahia's Outlook" was a relaxed but cooking homage to Charlie Parker. In conception it was a straight-ahead kicker that gave all the players ample room to show their stuff. Guest artist Pepper Adams was especially satisfying on the Parker original "Koko," which was offered at a blistering tempo. All the players, but especially Williams and Adams, were in solid command of their ideas. Even at rapid tempos the players managed to convey depth and nuance as they developed and pursued themes.

One for Bird contributed to Theresa's slow realization of a national identity and reputation; *Ed Kelly and Friend* finally put them on the map. Reviewer Gordon Raddue described Theresa's growing reputation in the following terms:

> Something almost scary is happening at Theresa Records, the strictly jazz operation launched three years ago by Allen, . . . the trumpet playing biological chemist. . . . Strange as it seems, Theresa is swiftly becoming one of the *world's top jazz labels*,

even though its catalogue, if that's the word, has only recently
creeped—or more accurately—exploded into double figures.
Originally devoted to outstanding Bay Area jazz figures . . .
Theresa's stock began zooming—figuratively at least—when
saxophonist Pharoah Sanders . . . joined the fold. (Raddue
1981, my emphasis)

Kazuko also remembered this critical period of Theresa's development in terms of the company's relationship to Pharoah;

None of it was planned . . . Pharoah is the main thing, I mean,
the fact that he got connected with us. If we hadn't made the
connection with him *we would be absolutely nowhere.* . . . I
mean I could show you graphs that back that up. . . . When
Pharoah's records came out, then everything else started selling too. (Kazuko 1981, my emphasis)

With a long silver and white beard, Pharoah Sanders was
a physically striking and painfully shy man with a genuine
and warm personality. His irrepressible southern roots combined with strong religious beliefs (he was a convert to Islam)
gave him a simple, often spiritual elegance. His talk was often
spare and direct. In 1959 Pharoah moved to the San Francisco
Bay area, from his native Little Rock, Arkansas, where he
had worked odd jobs, attended school, and kept his eyes and
ears open for music. While in the Bay area Pharoah developed
a reputation as a intense and serious jazz player. This intensity
remained a part of Pharoah's musical personality, as this description of his early years attests: "Pharoah was short, compact, and distrustful of any other sounds but music. He spoke
only with his eyes and with his tenor. His sound was a
squawking, screeching, top of the register explosion that in-

volved an extensive use of overtone series and overblowing of the horn" (Thomas 1975: 192).

After two and a half years in New York City, Pharoah returned to the Bay area, where he eventually met and later worked with the dominant saxophonist of the decade, John Coltrane.[2] Coltrane was drawn to the strength of Pharoah's musical personality and imagination. Coltrane found Pharoah

> a man of large spiritual reservoir. He's always trying to reach out to the truth. He's trying to allow his spiritual self to be his guide. He's dealing among other things, in energy, in integrity, in essences. I so much like the strength of his playing. Furthermore, he is one of the innovators and it's been my pleasure and privilege that he's been willing to help me, that he is part of the group. What I like about him is the strength of his playing, the conviction with which he plays. He has will and spirit and those are the qualities I like most in a man. (Simpkins 1975: 194).

This personal relationship between Pharoah and Coltrane culminated in Pharoah's joining Coltrane's band.

The association with Coltrane helped boost Pharoah's career. With Coltrane's help Pharoah secured a recording contract with Impulse!, where he produced a body of work that further enhanced his considerable reputation. The unexpected death of Coltrane in 1967 left Pharoah in line as one of the people most likely to continue the experimental and progressive direction started by Coltrane.

After five prolific years in the period immediately following Coltrane's death, Pharoah faded from public view even though by this time he had also developed a national following. By the late seventies, Pharoah's recording activity had all but disappeared. Resettled in Oakland, he occasionally performed at Bay area clubs with local musicians and friends. One of these friends, Ed Kelly, became the link between Theresa Records and Pharoah. According to Kazuko, "Ed Kelly brought him [Pharoah] over here and we just sat around and talked. . . . He said he got a good feeling, that he liked what was going on. . . . So he asked us if we'd be interested in recording him. . . . It was an evolving thing." (Kazuko 1981). This visit laid the groundwork that changed the direction of Theresa Records and Pharoah's career.

At the time of this meeting Pharoah was involved in a contract dispute with Arista Records. He was also coming off a disappointing commercial venture under his own name (*Think of One* on Artista) and a fusion collaboration with drummer Norman Connors. The collaborations with Conners were also commercial, designed to appeal to the pop market. While both projects generated some commercial exposure, they endeared themselves to some fans and confused others because the music was so different from Pharoah's collaborations with Coltrane as well as Pharoah's own material on Impulse! In any case, Pharoah was ready to leave Arista, but Pharoah's existing contract made joining Theresa difficult:

Sanders is currently in a contractual dispute with his label, Arista Records, which prevented Theresa from billing the jazz immortal more prominently on the record *Ed Kelly and Friend*—his name doesn't even appear on the front cover. "We've got to hope that either word gets around or that people are curious enough to flip the album over," says Allen. If Pharoah successfully gets out of his Arista deal, expect to see a sticker announcing his appearance on the album placed in some highly visible portion of the cover. (Jackson 1979: 10)

Kazuko's recollection of that period gives some indication of the chemistry that she, Allen, and Pharoah shared, as well as the change in their treatment by distributors:

> Pharoah's contract with Arista ran out and if given the choice he said *he would rather make music than money* and signed with us. . . . He's not exclusive. . . . We have an agreement to work together. With Pharoah the distributors became interested in us and wanted our products. So that's really when things started. (Kazuko 1981)

Pharoah's concern for aesthetic freedom was consistent with the developing perspective that Allen and Kazuko used to guide their first five records. Organizationally and ideologically Pharoah joined the close-knit social relations that had formed at Theresa. Not only did he bring visibility and a strong musical voice but he also brought with him a commitment to the music and the company.

The emerging relationship between Pharoah and Theresa also had lasting significance for Theresa in terms of its public identity and reputation. As Kazuko observed, after Pharoah's appearance on the label distributors not just were interested but aggressively pursued Theresa's records. As a Theresa recording artist, Pharoah helped give the label the exposure and credibility it sought.

Pharoah's Theresa debut came on *Ed Kelly and Friend* (TR106). Although this record was formally Kelly's date, the music on the record anticipated a certain pattern and thematic

approach to which Pharoah would return on subsequent recordings. Material in this and a subsequent Theresa session
provided anchors in a repertoire from which Pharoah would
repeatedly draw until 1986. Ballads and blues were all anchors
in the Kelly/Sanders book from which TR106 was drawn.

There were three Kelly originals on the date. "Rainbow
Song" was a slow, thoughtful ballad that was especially appropriate for the spiritual mood and personality of Sanders,
who played soprano saxophone. "You've Got to Have Freedom" and "Newborn" revealed the straight-ahead, blues-
based approach that continued to distinguish much of Pharoah's post-Coltrane work. Also notable, and a further antic-
ipation of a developing Sanders trademark, was his delicate
yet passionate approach to ballads (in this case "You Send
Me" and "Answer Me, My Love"). *Ed Kelly and Friend* was
essentially a quartet recording (the Ed Kelly trio plus Sanders).
Sanders and Kelly were joined by Peter Barshay on bass and
the tasteful Eddie Marshall on drums.

On the heels of *Ed Kelly and Friend* Allen and Kazuko
released TR107, entitled *Levels of Consciousness*, by drummer/
percussionist Babatunde and his band, Phenomena. *Levels of
Consciousness* was different in style and focus from anything
that Theresa released before or since. Not suprisingly the
record presented Theresa with distribution and promotion
problems precisely because it was so different from other
material in the catalogue. Distributors, retailers, and radio
stations had little idea how to promote this more commercial
pop album, in part because Theresa had established a clear
public reputation as a label whose music and artists were
committed to contemporary noncommercial acoustic jazz.
Distributors and retailers were familiar with Theresa's previous material; they knew where to stock and how to promote

it. The more commercial material posed a problem of promotion and efficiency because these same distributors and
retailers had little sense of Theresa's track record with this
more commercial music.

Part funk (inspired by R&B) and part fusion with some
message tunes, the record as a total idea was, at the time,
difficult to locate as jazz. The opening side featured the fusion
material, identifiable by driving rhythms and singable mel-
odies. The second side featured funk selections, including
several vocals concerned with love and brotherhood. Significantly the record maintained the practice of including nationally reputable artists: trombonist Julian Priester and
trumpeter Eddie Henderson were featured as guests.

The musical relationship between Theresa and Pharoah
was sealed with the release of *Journey to the One* (TR108/109).
In terms of conception, costs, studio time, and promotion
the project required a major allocation of Theresa's financial
and organizational resources. Because it was their most ambitious project to this point, the aesthetic and commercial
success of *Journey to the One* would have far-reaching consequences for members of the company and their future in
the record business. With this project Theresa found itself on
the threshold of the most significant period of its development
as a recording company.

Journey to the One featured Pharoah with Joe Bonner, Eddie
Henderson, and Idris Muhammad and various sized ensem-
bles. Released as a two-record set, the date captured the varied
sides of Pharoah's musical personality as Michael Ullman
described them in a *Boston Phoenix* (1981) review:

> Sanders plays "Easy to Remember" as if he were afraid to
> make a mistake. . . . "Kazuko" pairs Sanders with the slender

plaintive sound of the Japanese koto. . . . In all these recordings, Sanders plays his main instrument, the tenor saxophone.
. . . His repertoire has opened up suprisingly; he is playing
ballads and also Indian music and pieces influenced by the
Japanese. He seems to be neither straining after new worlds
to conquer, nor wallowing in nostalgia. He no longer shocks,
but remains unpredictable.

The release and critical acceptance of TR108/109 brought
Theresa a different set of pressures from those required to
get the company started. The record also brought the desired
increase in national exposure and cooperation by distributors.
This new public visibility and support by distributors, however, required consistent attention to the organization and
coordination of future projects as well as to distribution and
promotion. Since the company operated with the same sized
staff and resources, the routine but critical financial and organizational responsibilities associated with the manufacture
and distribution of records (coordinating tours, booking acts,
covering radio stations and promotion, etc.) sometimes assumed monumental proportions. Allen and Kazuko faced
new pressures, which required consistent attention to all facets
of the operation.

The release of *Journey to the One* also marked the end of
Theresa's formative stages of development. With Pharoah on
the label (and the cumulative affect of their previous releases)
the company was no longer just a local or even a regional
company. Although it remained very much a small independent jazz recording company, its reach and impact now far
surpassed its size. And the public identity and reputation that
had been achieved through the release of *Journey to the One*
were solidified by the two records that followed.

That Kazuko, Allen, and Paul now knew how to make the kind of records they wanted became obvious with TR110 and TR111. *Kabsha* (TR110) by drummer Idris Muhammad was satisfying in conception and presentation. The session was remarkable because it presented two major tenor saxophone players, Pharoah Sanders and George Coleman, in a quartet led by Muhammad on drums with Ray Drummond on bass. (The absence of a piano in such a quartet was unusual.) The session's major disappointment was that Sanders and Coleman appeared together only on the opening selection, a showcase interaction entitled "GCCG Blues." On the remaining material, Pharoah or Coleman led trios through ballads and straight-ahead, blues-based tunes, enhanced by the restrained though provocative performance of Idris Muhammad, who approached the instrument with a tasteful mix of power and swing. Highlights of the session included "GCCG Blues," "Little Feet" with George Coleman, and "I Want to Talk About You," featuring Pharoah. Two notices give some idea of the enthusiasm with which this record was received around the country:

Two new ones from that fine Bay area label, Theresa, are always welcome on the heels of Pharoah Sanders' excellent comeback on that label. With those two new additions to their catalogue I'm sold on this label. (Jenkins 1981)

And from *Klacto Jazz Magazine:*

This independent California label continues its fine release record with the addition of these two straight-ahead successes. The Muhammad date is a robust one, with Idris' percussive talents coming to the forefront. . . . Of course with the help of two such formidable saxophonists as Coleman and Sanders, and the thick resonant sound of Drummond's bass, its hard not to hear anything but the best that jazz can offer.

Perpetual Stroll by bassist Rufus Reid (TR111) achieved the conceptual possibilities initially suggested by Ed Kelly's *Music from the Black Museum*. It also anticipated conceptual directions that were later realized on Joe Bonner's *Impressions of Copenhagen* (TR114). Eddie Gladden on drums and Kirk Lightsey at the piano joined bassist Reid to complete the trio. The record was clear in conception and clean in execution. Both qualities were due to the command of the players and the chemistry they generated as former members of Dexter Gordon's rhythm section. As a unit these players suggested, anticipated, and listened carefully to all the ideas on the table. They contributed to and altered those ideas as they saw fit, trusting each other's contribution and judgment. This record ranked among Theresa's most impressive releases in conception, production quality, and execution. The material on the date was a mixture of original compositions by Lightsey as well as jazz standard by Herbie Hancock and Oscar Pettiford.

W. A. Brower's review in *Jazz Times* gives some indication of critical responses to *Perpetual Stroll*:

> If I can hazard a rather grand perspective "Perpetual Stroll" is what an album should be about from the point of view of jazz's historical integrity. Its raison d'etre is to document a worthy creative moment. . . . Each player is an artist. Each brings a personal expressiveness to their particular instrument. Obviously three such talented players go into a studio without knowing each other and make a smoking record. It's been done before. But it's unlikely they'd produce a "Perpetual

Stroll" that way. . . . There are no accidents here. The execution is stunning. They make listening to a ballad or a waltz
a fresh experience again. (Brower 1981)

By the release of *Rejoice* (TR112/113), Pharoah's second
album, Theresa's status as a reputable jazz label was fully
established. Aesthetically and in terms of production quality,
Rejoice was even more ambitious and completely realized than
its predecessor, *Journey to the One*. Although its commercial
impact did not equal its aesthetic and critical success, the
record expressed in music and feeling Theresa's public identity
as a record company.

The musicians featured were a comment on the respectability and reach of both Pharoah and Theresa. In various
sessions were drummers Elvin Jones and Billy Higgins, pianists Joe Bonner and John Hicks, bassist Art Davis, vibra-
phonist Bobby Hutcherson. Danny Moore, Steve Turre,
Babatunde, Lois Colin, and George Johnson also appeared.
The music included standards by John Coltrane and Benny
Carter, as well as several Sanders originals, including two
West African–influenced highlife tunes. The music was also
presented in a variety of settings—duets, quartets, quintets.
The music on this record was primarily a showcase for the
spirit and musicianship of Sanders. The moods ranged from
festive celebration ("Rejoice," "Highlife," "Nigerian Juju Hil-
ife") to relaxed contemplation ("When Lights Are Low,"
"Central Park West"). Sanders' playing ranges from muscular
agility ("Origin," "Moment's Notice") to delicate sensitivity
("Farah" and "Ntjilo Ntjilo").

In retrospect Allen conceded that perhaps there was too
much material included on this record and that its costs got

out of hand. These observations say as much about Allen and Kazuko's naiveté in the record business as it does about their commitment to Pharoah, his music, and the kind of record company they wanted. From a purely business standpoint, the material on this record might have been more econom-ically presented as two records. (Indeed, the two records [TR116/TR118] released by Sanders immediately after *Rejoice* were for the most part restatements and reinterpretations of the material from the *Rejoice* session.) However, the signif-icance of the record and the experience in Theresa's evolution and Pharoah's career would have been lost if it had been issued as two records.

Press and critical notices for the record were vigorous in their support; distributors became respectful rather than merely tolerant as they had been in Theresa's early years. Kazuko described this change in attitude:

> Distributors will pay you on the basis of how well your records are selling. Since we've been dealing with Pharoah his records sell, so they [distributors] want them. They [distributors] know that to get it [the record] they have to pay. They have to pay their previous bills to get more records from us and that's the way it works. Oh! They're paying now. Sure, . . . in fact the guy at Richmond Brothers [Theresa's former distributor in New York, Philadelphia, New Jersey, and Washington D.C.] says, "We enjoy doing business with you, your records sell." (Kazuko 1981).

Allen, Kazuko, and Paul saw this change in attitude by distributors as a sign of their legitimacy in the industry. How-ever, with this new legitimacy came a new set of problems:

Paul: People [radio stations, distributors] are happy to get Theresa records. They write us and say, "I haven't heard anything new from you in two months. Where's your new release?"
Allen: It's like anything else, unless you start out with Dexter Gordon, Pharoah, or Miles or somebody that people know. That was our mistake. We had to go begging with these records, "Oh please play these records, you don't have to pay me just take 'em."
Kazuko: Well it went from the problems of getting the distributors to take the records. . . . Now it's more they take them but they don't pay for them. . . . Or pay for them when they feel like it. (Allen, Kazuko, Paul 1981)

Thus, with industry, critical, and public recognition Theresa's difficulties shifted from getting exposure for their records to getting paid. The problem of timely payments plagues small firms; obviously, cash flow is crucial to their ability to develop and produce new products and to continue to have a presence in the marketplace.

By 1982, Theresa's public reputation and legitimacy as a national manufacturer of jazz records was firmly established. In its formative years four of its seven records featured the work of nationally recognized artists. After the release of *Journey to the One* all Theresa's releases featured nationally recognized artists. After *Rejoice* came a live record by Pharoah called *Live* (TR116) and two solid recordings by pianists Joe Bonner—*Impressions of Copenhagen* (TR114)—and John Hicks—*Some Other Time* (TR115).

The latter two continued directions first anticipated by *Ed Kelly and Friend* and later realized in Reid's *Perpetual Stroll.* Bonner's outing was a lush and romantic reading of the sights and sounds of Denmark. Augmented by strings, bells, and chimes the record was significant as much for its compositional unity and conception as for Bonner's performance. *Some Other Time* had Hicks in trio with two members of Theresa's musical family—Idris Muhammad on drums and Walter Booker on bass. Side one was a suite, or more accurately a group, of loosely connected Hicks originals. Side two ventured into compositions by other composers, among them Hicks' contemporary George Cables. The material was wide in its reach and performed with intensity and acuity. Both records were focused as well as full and clean in their sound. These recordings represented the work of a stable and maturing Theresa Records.

By 1983 there was no clearer signal of the musical maturation and respectability of Theresa Records than the formation of a musical relationship with Nat Adderley and his band. This relationship led to the release of *On the Move with the Nat Adderley Quintet* (TR117). This energetic date was recorded live in San Francisco with Sonny Fortune, Larry Willis, Jimmy Cobb, Walter Booker, and Adderley. The record achieved the feeling and excitement of a working unit rather than a momentary collaboration full of musicianship but devoid of essence. Like the Rufus Reid session (TR111) these players were able to translate musical and social relationships into forceful and interesting musical ideas.

Between 1983 and 1986, Theresa also issued numbers TR118–TR122. This set of releases included new material from Pharoah: *Heart Is a Melody* and *Shukuru* (TR118 and TR121). From John Hicks came a thoughtful set of solo, duet, and trio performances called *John Hicks* (TR119). In 1985,

Theresa released *Manhattan Panorama* (TR120), an occasionally satirical but intense session by George Coleman. The
company completed this scattered round of releases in 1986
with *Blue Autumn* (TR122) by the Nat Adderley Quintet,
which included the remaining material recorded during the
live session issued as TR117.

While the company's public reputation continued to grow
with each new release and each new musician's association
with the label, things were not as smooth as they appeared
organizationally and financially. Although the records between TR117 an TR122 certainly maintained and enhanced
Theresa's reputation for quality and integrity, and frequency
of releases in this period slowed to one recording a year.
Moreover, the released material was either recorded live
(TR116, TR117) or was previously recorded material (TR122)
that remained unreleased awaiting capital to finance production. No doubt, some of Theresa's problems were internal,
but many were not. In its period of greatest aesthetic recognition and legitimacy as a significant independent voice,
Theresa also faced the sometimes severe constraints of small
independent recording companies—distribution problems,
cash flow problems, a slowdown in record sales, increases in
production costs, ambitious projects, and budget overruns.
Where Theresa's initial focus on Bay area musicians meant
that it could operate with limited contact with distributors
and radio stations, its evolution to a nationally recognized
company meant greater organizational and financial demands,
responsibilities, and constraints. The constraints shifted from
getting artists and records exposure in the press and on the
radio to getting distributors to push the records and pay their

bills on time. The consequences of these new problems were felt most dramatically in the kinds of creative projects Theresa could produce and the pace of getting that material out.

The problems of being a jazz independent notwithstanding, by 1986 Theresa Records was a different company in terms of identity, reputation, and legitimacy. The transition to a national company and the ongoing relationship with its original artists and those with wide reputations helped to shape the identity and direction of the company. Although they encountered problems, Allen and Kazuko nevertheless emerged with a stronger and clearer conception of themselves, their artists, their company, and the kind of music they wanted to make.

MAKING RECORDS AND GETTING PAID: INDEPENDENT DISTRIBUTION

If they're [distributors] not into the music . . . they're not going to do a good job. They may try to sell a Pharoah Sanders record but they won't try to sell a John Hicks record . . . That's going to mean that the product is going to sit on their shelves . . . and they are not going to want to pay Allen.

Duncan Browne, Rounder Distribution, March 1987

In spite of their ideological and aesthetic autonomy independent firms must constantly negotiate and manage a production and distribution system that limits and shapes their work. Unless Theresa could generate a consistent and reliable track record, a stable of marketable products, and a public identity as a jazz recording company, it faced distribution problems. Early in its development, the external problem of record distribution was a major constraint. Once it established a track record within the industry and with the public, the particular source and expression of the external constraints it faced remained. They shifted slightly from the problems of establishing a track record as a consistent and reliable company to the need for enough new products, innovation, and sales to generate the cash flow necessary to remain in the marketplace. Theresa had to maintain enough sales to continue to finance new projects, without which the financial solvency of the company would be threatened. Without financial solvency and the access to money to continue to make records the company's stability would be threatened. Because of its small size and limited resources, Theresa continually faced the twin pressures of generating new material and paying for existing projects.

These organizational and financial problems were rooted in the structure of the independent distribution system. The built-in constraints of independent distribution are often passed on to small recording companies, which because of size, location, and type of music are least able to manage such constraints. Ultimately, passing along the structural contradictions of the system affects the creation of art and culture, especially the range of cultural choices available to the public. At the same time that Theresa's distribution system limited its autonomy, it made that autonomy possible.

Environmental Turbulence

Richard Peterson and David Berger used the concept of entrepreneurship to describe the organizational forms employed by record companies to manage the demands of the highly competitive and unstable popular music market (1971). They referred to this instability as "turbulence" and suggested that the unpredictable nature of a popular music market built on demographic characteristics and tastes results in specific external and internal pressures on culture-producing organizations. These pressures require that organizations develop routine methods of creating, manufacturing, and distributing their products in order to minimize the impact of this turbulence.

The turbulence that Peterson and Berger identified stems from periodic shifts in the composition of ownership in the music industry and control over markets. With this turbulence, they suggested, came "a host of independents unfettered by organizational complexities, who formed their own companies and in a few years ended the predominance of large established corporations" (1971). Historically, increased competition from independents provoke attempts by major companies to reduce or eliminate the market instability created by the proliferation of firms in the market. Major companies use a number of organizational and financial strategies to weaken or eliminate their smaller competitors. For instance, during the sixties majors increased the use of freelance producers, many of whom were directly involved with musicians responsible for major stylistic innovations that swept the industry in the 1940s and 1950s (Gillett 1972; Shaw 1978). Major companies also stepped up their acquisitions of small companies. With some of these they formed subsidiary labels and divisions within their existing structure; others they withdrew from the market (Chapple and Garofalo 1977; Denisoff 1975).

The majors also extend control over the distribution and retail outlets, specifically in the form of wholly owned retail and distribution operations. Major companies also regularly influence significant gatekeepers (press, video, radio) who operate in the popular music business with press junkets and various complimentary gifts (Chapple and Garofalo 1977; Frith 1981). While radio is still the primary means of exposure for independents (especially college, community, and public radio in the case of jazz), the attention given to their products in the press and on commercial radio does not approach the levels enjoyed by major companies.

Regardless of the size or scale of the firm, it is clear from the evidence that firms operating in turbulent conditions such as the popular music industry attempt to reduce the degree of instability and unpredictability by stabilizing and where possible extending their control over the external and internal sources of the turbulence. For Theresa the major source of external turbulence was its distribution system.

The Distribution System for Theresa Records

Most of Theresa's internal problems such as cash flow, organizational stability, and production scheduling were related to the broader issue of distribution. At an independent like Theresa making records is easy, but getting them to the public can be next to impossible (Ryan and Peterson 1982). In searching for an answer to how and why this is so, I found Theresa's greatest source of frustration and their greatest latitude for innovation and autonomy to be distribution.

The independent distribution system within which Theresa operated is replete with people, organizations, practices, and an internal logic that must be managed for records to reach the public. Throughout this distribution system various organizations and actors are constrained by demands, interests, and ideologies that do not always coincide.

Theresa's northeastern distributor was Rounder Distribution, an arm of the Rounder Organization, which also operated Rounder Records. Both the record label and the distribution service grew out of the desire of bluegrass enthusiasts to get bluegrass music on record and to relevant audiences during a period in which there was a general lack of interest in bluegrass music in the industry. In 1972, Rounder Records and later Rounder Distribution were formed. Duncan Browne, head of Rounder Distribution, oversaw an operation that distributed records, cassettes, and compact discs for over four hundred independent labels. In his late twenties and with the Rounder organization for eight years, the fast-talking Browne was energetic and had a cynical but good-humored view of the independent music business.

As Browne (1987) described it, the contemporary system of independent record distribution has not changed very much in the last half-decade. The major change has been the subtle shift in emphasis and the escalating economic resources required to promote and distribute records. For a company like Rounder Distribution (and inevitably for a firm like Theresa), this means that the distribution process operates in a system of social relations where the economic interests of the various members are not always the same. Moreover, the constraints facing different participants are sometimes multiple and contradictory.

For starters, this is Browne's rather compressed description of the distribution process used by Theresa Records:

Let's say Theresa lets us know they've got a new John Hicks record coming out. We have a number of sales people who work for the company who give their input as to what we estimate we would sell on a given record, based on their knowledge of their accounts [retail stores] and their estimation of what their accounts will want. We then put together an order; hopefully we combine input from as many sales people as possible and our own previous experience with other products by that artist or similar types of products. We put together an order and we call that into Theresa. Theresa ships us "x" number of units; we get them in; they get put into informational paperwork that we give to our sales people and then send out to retail stores and so forth (Brown 1987).

Although this description is greatly simplified, it indicates that independent distributors must mediate between competing and often opposed interests—those of the retailers (their own accounts) and those of the record label.

The interests and constraints facing these three components of the distribution system seem to converge only in the most general sense and in the most ideal of circumstances. These interests converge around the mutual financial stakes in the successful sale of independent music. Because the retailers, record labels, and distributors operate at different locations in the music industry, even the most ideal social and economic relationships still move between cooperation and conflict. The independent distributor's central location in the system of independent recording is key to understanding under what circumstances different interests converge, when they do not, and how these shifts affect Theresa's operation.

The Relationship Between the Distributor and Retailer

Contemporary jazz independents like Theresa operate in a changing retail environment. The changes are in part the result of new audio technology and partly the result of changes in the nature of record retail outlets. Large retail discount houses and record store chains have increasingly replaced privately owned record stores. These large chains deal in volume with commercially popular records. Quick sales and volume are both the arena of majors rather than independents.

The critical and commercial success of the compact disc has also affected the independent record manufacturer and distributor. For major firms it is economically profitable to manufacture compact discs because these companies operate on a large enough scale and in large enough volume to hold down production costs. These companies experience higher rates of return on their investments with this new technology because the discs can be manufactured and sold in sufficient quantities to guarantee profitability. For small independents like Theresa, on the other hand, the costs of releasing material on compact disc as opposed to albums or cassette tapes are prohibitive because the scale of operation is too small and the independent's markets too limited. Hence Theresa and many other independents still operate mainly in album format. The constraints from these organizational and technological developments are particularly tight for independents both because it is increasingly difficult for some independent companies to get their records into retail outlets and because, once in the store, the record often receives insufficient space or attention from the retailers (Goodman 1987: J6).

Regardless of a firm's size, organization, ideology, products, or location in the recording industry, independent distribution in general is constrained by space, resource limitations, and competition from other distributors. To appreciate the potency and range of these constraints, consider that Rounder Distribution alone handled products for over four hundred labels. This means that they were always trying to sell between twenty-five and fifty new records a week. Although this scale seems large for a single distributor, compared to other larger independent distributors and majors it was less than 1 percent of the new music released weekly.

The pressures and competition are increased by the limited opportunities available to jazz independents for public exposure (radio airplay, media coverage, advertising space, retail space). The main response, especially by large manufacturers and distributors of popular music, is to fill these limited spaces with records that are familiar and predictable and that are quick sellers. The sellers of such spaces seek rapid turnover to increase the earning power of the space. In the competitive commercial music market, less well-known independent musics cost these sellers more than commercial music (Chapple and Garofalo 1977; Denisoff 1975; Frith 1981).

The organization of the popular music consumers into general categories based on demographic characteristics and buying habits is designed specifically to minimize the risks involved in making available records that appeal to these identifiable segments. This organizational strategy also helps distributors to reach these preferred audiences quickly and efficiently. Along with the precise organization of markets, overproduction is the basic industry response to the inherent uncertainties that accompany constant changes in the market (Frith 1981). Sales was one of the key departments at Rounder Distribution where these constraints were felt directly and managed. Record sales were handled by a small sales staff that maintained direct contact with Rounder Distribution's retail accounts.

Large major companies, on the other hand, depend on a

core of stable retail accounts to place large orders for popular-selling records; this approach works because the majors can effectively create visibility and popularity for their records. Large retailers (where volume and genre are not really issues) are willing to enter into stable relationships with them because the burden of generating demand falls on the producer rather than on the retail outlet. Thus large retailers depend on the products of majors for their profits. In this relationship successful record sales depend not so much on the retailer's knowledge of the music as on the label's control of and access to large, stable markets. Major distributors and record labels also influence retailers through their economic and organizational power. As Browne pointed out,

> Most distributors of independent music do not come into a retail buyer and shove stuff down their throat. A CBS salesman comes in, or a Polygram salesman, or whatever, comes in and they will frequently sit down with a buyer and say, "You have to take 'x' number and in order to encourage you to do so I will give you ten percent advertising, ten percent free goods, you can take three months to pay me. (Browne 1987)

In this situation the influence exerted by major companies comes from their control over resources (e.g., advertising, distribution, records, perks, credit, and payment schedules).

In contrast, Rounder depended more on a negotiated sales strategy since they could exert limited economic and organizational leverage. According to Browne this negotiated approach depended heavily on the knowledge of sales staff and their relationship to the retail account. Both the retailer's and the salesperson's sense of the market, customer interest, and tastes played a direct role in sales.

> Independent distributors, generally speaking, know what the account can sell, know what the buyer is interested in, know the demographics that the specific account is dealing in. He will come in and say, "Here are the new jazz records, you do well in jazz. . . . What do you want?" putting the onus to buy or not to buy on the buyer.
>
> We [Rounder Distribution] don't have the tools to force anybody to buy anything. So we have to rely on our knowledge of the account, the market base, and the product to be able to force the buyer's attention on specific things (Browne 1987).

As described by Browne this more negotiated character of sales was no doubt the result of the structural location of distributor and retailers. But it also makes sense ideologically. That is, the account offered by Browne is materially rooted in the nature of Rounder's work and how it managed its constraints. As I've noted, the key factor in the coordination and organization of Rounder Distribution's sales was the staff's knowledge of and rapport with their retail accounts. The staff must learn how to sell records to their accounts, they must know the products, they must know the audience. Browne's job was to coordinate and monitor these relationships. He made sure that members of his staff were not distracted by competing accounts or the pressures to build new accounts. His objective was to maximize the rapport between retailer and salesperson since there were a limited number of levers that could be exerted by Rounder on the retailer.

Time also shaped the work of the sales staff. Most sales

at Rounder Distribution were made through a combination of personal visits and telephone contacts. With definite time limitations, a large catalogue of independent music, and a steady flow of new releases, sales personnel must not only know their accounts and the markets they service, but also know the artists and the music they sell. In a quick stacatto delivery, Browne described the time constraints faced by his sales staff:

> You only have "x" amount of time with the buyer and twenty-five to fifty records a week is a lot. It [a record description] takes more than a minute apiece so you have have to prepick your shots. A lot of our sales are phone sales. You have to pick your shots especially on the phone. Fifteen minutes on the phone is a long time and the average sales call is not even fifteen minutes. So you've got to say in fifteen minutes this guy is going to want to reorder all of the stuff he sold in the past week, plus I've got to tell him about all the new releases, so in advance of the call you look at the new releases and you'll say, okay here are the ones that are a must, here are the ones that this account will really have to have, and then if I have time we'll go on to the other things (Browne 1987).[1]

All distributors face similar constraints stemming from the limitations of time, competition, differences in power, resources, and market position. Independent distributors like Rounder are limited because the types of music they distribute are not popular (in the sense of reaching large commercial markets), widely promoted, or commercially accessible: often retailers are skeptical about the appeal of the music and, as a consequence, they are sometimes apprehensive about establishing relationships with independent labels and distributors.

Browne regarded such skepticism as an opportunity: "The approach that we take to independent distribution is we want to be the "one-stop" source for independent music. So that a store can say, 'Oh, it's some weird independent record, it must come from Rounder.' That's the headset" (Browne 1987). It was in Rounder Distribution's responses to the needs of the retailer (and as we'll see the record label) that it functioned as mediator between the small labels and the retailers. More important, in this mediator role Rounder tried to incorporate and yet minimize the uncertainties of independent music for both retailers and labels. They turned idiosyncracies into assets. They became specialists in managing the aesthetic and organizational uncertainties of independent music.

> We've been here for fifteen years. . . . We've tried to establish ourselves as, "Yeah, we're a bunch of fruitcake flakes with weirdo tastes in music," but we can make it possible for John Q Retail record store to deal with all this weirdo flake music and maybe attract a fairly secure, reliable, consistent clientele that will come to your store to find product because they know you'll have this weirdo stuff as well as having the Bruce Springsteen. So you may get the cat who wants the Pharoah Sanders record plus he wants to buy whatever [perhaps a more esoteric artist than Sanders] and so that's what we try to offer. It is a service where you can deal with this stuff fairly worry-free with people who have their business shit together. (Browne 1987)

Thus, Rounder's location, organization, and operation shaped and constrained its ability to sell records to retailers. In this system of independent record distribution such constraints and frustrations are passed on to the weakest members of the system—the small independent labels. How do these organizational and economic arrangements affect Theresa Records?

Relationship Between the Record Distributor and the Record Label

Structurally the independent record distributor occupies perhaps the most pivotal position in the system of independent music. The commercial success of a record depends, in part, on its public exposure and the timing of that exposure. Once the promotional machinery (radio and video airplay, record reviews, advertising, club and concert appearances) is activated, quick and easy access to the music by the public is critical to its commercial success.

How and when the music of Theresa's artists made it to the public depended on the relationship between the distributor and the retailer I have been describing. It also depended on the relationship between the company and its distributors, especially their mutual cooperation in recording records and paying outstanding bills. Because the environment where producers, buyers, and sellers of independent music operate is so precarious, retailers worry especially about the long-term stability of the recording label, the commercial potential of the music, and most efficient way to buy and sell independent music. In the persona of a record retailer, Browne described the uncertainties faced by retailers and distributors and how their strategy to minimize these risks directly affected Theresa Records:

Is the company going to be in business tomorrow? Am I going to buy this product and if I don't sell it what's going to happen? If I take in a Pharoah Sanders record tomorrow is Theresa going to be around? If I'm dealing with Theresa I don't know that. If I'm dealing with distributor "X" who's been here for twenty years, distributor "X" will do it. If they don't I'm going to tell them that I'm not going to pay the bill.

Now, Theresa, I only owe them a hundred bucks. If I'm buying from Theresa and Black Saint and India Navigation and so on so I owe five hundred people a hundred bucks; that's a lot of dough—I owe fifty thousand. But it's all a hundred dollars here, here, and here and these guys may come and go tomorrow.

But if I'm dealing with one source [an independent distributor] for all those labels and I owe them fifty thousand dollars, you can be damn sure they're gonna take care of this stuff [payment] because they wanna see most of their fifty thousand. So if Theresa goes out of business tomorrow, it doesn't matter; they're gonna take the records back. I don't have to worry about them. As the retailer I'm gonna pay them [the distributor] everything I owe them (Browne 1987).

Allen experienced the consequences of this system directly, and clearly the major consequence was economic. "When you put out one record [a year] the money you get in comes very slowly. We may make forty or fifty thousand bucks in a year. . . . [But] I'm constantly going in the hole financially" (interview, 1987). Problems of payment are also compounded by the sudden disappearance of a distributor. In fact Allen and Kazuko recounted at least two stories of bankruptcy of major independent distributors with whom they'd tied up records and money.

Another consequence of the distribution system felt internally at the level of the record company is the lack of consistent and aggressive sales by its distributors. In a typical example, one of Theresa's midwestern distributors did not seem to push the products as hard as Allen believed it should. Allen subsequently approached a larger, more established distributor that was thought to be reputable and that because of its size, was also thought to have access to a larger variety of retail outlets.

Allen's account of his ordeal with this distributor is insightful. It captures both his eternal optimism and the routine frustrations of dealing with the independent distribution system:

> There was one big distributor in Minnesota. . . . I went to him because I heard he had this connection with one of the major chains and that he could possibly move a lot of records. I also heard from other people that it is hard to get money out of him, that he's a nice guy but you could never get ahold of him and that he is having some money problems. I mean he only ordered thirty each of Pharoah and fifty of George's and I haven't seen a cent and I haven't heard from him at all. If he doesn't pay for those I'm not going to send him any more records. I figure he's got problems and I don't need his problems. (Allen 1987)

This example also illustrates Browne's contention that in the larger context and environment of independent distribution a small company like Theresa is often seen by large multiline distributors as dispensable. Indeed Browne blamed both the labels and the distributors for this state of affairs. For him both were parties to a relationship that was defined by constantly escalating miscommunication and economic pressures between label, retailer, and distributor. This situation led to a downward spiral of insensitivity, irresponsibility, and frustration.

> If they're [distributors] not into the music, they're not going to give a shit and they're not going to do a good job. They may try to sell a Pharoah Sanders record, but they won't try to sell a John Hicks record. Nat Adderley maybe, maybe not. . . . That's going to mean that the product is going to sit on their shelves and that's going to mean that they are not going to want to pay Allen because they're going to want to go check the inventory and they're going to say, "What the hell, we've got a thousand records, forget it. We're not going to pay this guy—we owe him five thousand dollars."
> So he's [Allen] not going to see a cash flow. He's going to get bummed out about the distributor. He's going to give up communicating with the distributor. The distributor's going to think that the label's not happening. . . . and you've got a debacle. (Browne 1987).

The root of this escalating miscommunication and unresponsiveness is, in the final analysis, economic. It stems from the absence of record sales. Small independent labels no less than distributors depend on sales to maintain their operations. Distributors do not sell records properly and effectively, according to Browne, because they don't know how, because they often lack the appropriate resources, because they are often not interested, and because independent labels do not offer much guidance and support. In a distribution system based on sales these factors often work against smaller, weaker, and more precarious operations like Theresa. These companies simply do not have the resources to get their products to the public and once there to compete with larger, more resourceful companies.

Browne regarded Rounder Distribution's organization as an effective approach to managing and containing the constraints that are built into this system. But an organized and responsible independent distributor is not enough. Independent labels must constantly badger, educate, and direct the distributor in the nuances of their music and their artists. Browne suggested that independent labels (like the distributor in relationship to the retailer) must make it easy for the distributor to sell their records. How? By keeping the distributor informed. The distributor's response is then:

> Well, here's a piece of paper about all the shit that's going on with this guy. I'd better run out and tell all the stores about it. We'll get some orders and all of a sudden I see some product turn and all of a sudden Allen calls up for some dough and I look at the shelves and see "gee, the product is turning." I should send him some dough because if I don't I'm not going to get any more product to sell which seems to be selling. (Browne 1987)

The assumption here is that both the recording label and the distributor have mutual stakes in the sale of records. The relationship between the label and the distributor is jeopardized when, for whatever reason, records do not sell. The relationship between distributor and record label is further threatened by the structural circumstances of jazz as a commercial product and the location of independent firms in the broader complex of the popular music industry. Where any one of these relationships break down or the economic interests on which they are based are threatened, then conflicts emerge.

In the case of independent music in general and jazz in particular, difficulties of the kind experienced by Theresa emerge not so much because independent music is so different or so unsellable but because distributors are not always enthusiastic or do not have the interest of their labels in mind. According to the logic of this distribution system the retailers and distributors first meet the needs of the stronger, more resourceful companies. Their bills get paid on time. Their orders are filled and refilled promptly. That the system operates in this way has less to do with the quality of the music as with each party's attempt to maintain economic and organizational control over the resources required to get products through the production and distribution system consistently.

The financial impact of this relationship between distributor and label was felt directly by Theresa. The collective weight of debts (from distributors) owed to Theresa added up. At any given moment five to ten accounts owed Theresa $5,000–6,000 apiece. According to Allen, this meant that the company was owed $40,000–50,000 "all the time." In the routine business of modern recording firms $50,000 is not a lot of money. However, for a firm like Theresa, which may spend $20,000 per project, $50,000 might well be the difference between doing two or three projects per year.

Consider, for instance, the production costs for a project

like *Shukuru* (TR121). Up to the stage where the records are actually manufactured, Allen claimed, it is difficult to complete projects for under $20,000:

> It's hard to do [a project] for less than twenty [thousand] anymore. If you think of four people, side men may get fifteen hundred dollars and the artists [leader] may get, it depends on the artists, around five thousand dollars. He may get more, maybe less. But you're talking about ten grand there. Studio costs? A couple of thousand on studio at least; twenty or twenty-five, or three thousand for tape. There's mastering and that's maybe another thousand and its starts running up. You can get to twenty [thousand] easily. (Allen 1986)

Beyond these studio and production expenses are manufacturing costs. These include expenses necessary for pressing the records, printing (including the jackets and inserts), publicity, and promotion ("you've got to figure that I give away about fifteen hundred to two thousand records"), as well as shipping. Artist and mechanical royalties together add another $1.40 to the cost of each record. According to Allen, these post-production expenses add another $10,000 to the cost of the project.

With these kinds of costs I asked Allen how many records must be sold for him to break even and recoup his investments.

> Let's say you spend $30,000. . . . Let's say you make two dollars a record. That's . . . fifteen thousand records [sales]. Most albums would be way off that [in terms of sales]. I'm really worried about getting my costs back. Even just the pressing costs. Like this Nat Adderley record [TR122] is being

pressed and I'm just pressing four thousand. I'll get a bill for six thousand bucks here shortly and these records could sit around the house for a month. It's going to be a long time before I start getting some of that money back. And, as I say, [with] that plus the other costs, you've got to try to get back about ten grand or so for production costs. (Allen 1986)

Given Theresa's organizational size and financial resources it is easy to see how even the slightest interruption in cash flow could seriously disrupt its ability to produce records. In addition to the constant threat to the company's organizational stability, the nickel and dime approach to payment by distributors sapped energy and produced frustration, disappointment, and a growing lack of confidence in the system of independent distribution. This sense of frustration, disappointment, and disillusionment was repeatedly echoed in Allen and Kazuko's account of their experiences.

Thus, the size and resources of a record company do matter significantly in its ability to remain financially solvent. Size and resources also matter in the kinds of records that get made and the company's ability to get them to the public. As we've seen, when faced with a situation of delinquent accounts and in some cases nonpayment by distributors, large companies (both independents and majors) exert a certain leverage in their relationship to retailers and distributors. Because of organizational and economic resources these companies can threaten to withhold new or additional records (or terminate the relationship completely) until delinquent accounts are paid.

In theory all record labels, regardless of size, can potentially use such leverage. However, the leverage that Allen could exert on distributors was not always available nor so clearly expressed. Allen's leverage was more indirect. It was expressed more in terms of negotiations based on long-term relationships: "The distributors that have been in there long enough, you know, they will pay. Like I just called three of them and I said I need some money for production costs. Even though they hadn't ordered any records you use that as a kind of leverage and you can just tell them. If you've been working with somebody long enough you feel like you ought to be able to call them and tell them to pay something on their bill and generally they'll do it without any hassle" (Allen 1986). In those cases where there was little basis for negotiation or distributors were simply uncooperative and unresponsive Allen threatened to withhold orders or break off the relationship completely (as he did with the midwestern distributor).

Regardless of which strategy was employed, the leverage Allen could exert was limited and conditional. First, since the demand for Theresa's records was limited, unless Theresa had a really successful record—a hit—distributors could afford to string the company along indefinitely. Second, because some of the distributors that handled Theresa's product also handled products from many other labels, the impact (both short and long term) of the disappearance of Theresa's product from a distributor's line would be negligible. This combination of limited sales, limited interest in Theresa's products by retailers and distributors, and the marginal structural position of both independent labels and independent distributors contributed to Allen's continual frustrations.[2]

Allen tried to manage these uncertainties and soften their impact in several ways.[3] As I show in Chapter Five, one source of considerable debate in the company was whether or not to broaden its aesthetic scope and release more commercial music (e.g., fusion). This strategy was not fully explored because it threatened the public reputation and identity of the company. In terms of distribution this strategy also created as many problems as it solved since it might easily strain the effectiveness of Theresa's existing distribution system. The company's current distributors would have to cultivate a new network of retailers, radio stations, and promotional outlets. Along with these ideological and organizational problems the most serious questions involved the uncertainties that come with exploring new territory.

In contrast to this flirtation with more commercial material Allen and Kazuko pursued a different strategy. In fact, this response was not so much a deliberate strategy to deal with the uncertainties of independent distribution as an adjustment required to keep the company solvent. Once it reached the national stage of its development, Theresa began systematically to limit the number of records it released annually (although not necessarily the number of projects explored). In addition, by the mid-1980s it began releasing material recorded live and already "in the can." This strategy was a way to reduce production costs and the already serious strain on its resources. The strategy kept Theresa's artists in the public eye while maintaining the company's reputation.

Finally and most significantly, the company was able to remain financially solvent and aesthetically active through a licensing arrangement that allowed a European firm to manufacture and market Theresa Records in Europe. This deal proved key to the company's ability to keep its artists and records before the public, though in a reduced and limited form. In the face of delinquent payments by distributors this agreement provided the company with a sorely needed base of operating capital, allowing Allen and Kazuko to soften the impact of their uncertain environment. According to Allen, "The licensing deal bought me out of the slump because I was really getting disgusted with the whole thing. I couldn't sell anything in Europe. All that changed immediately as soon as I signed this thing" (Allen 1986).

This licensing deal allowed Allen and Kazuko to shift some of the financial risks of several records to the holder of the license: "They [the licensing company] come up with some money up front every year. What they give me is just an advance on royalties. I send them a copy of the mastertape and the negatives from the jacket covers. They press the records and print the cover with a little thing [indicating] the holder of the license. They pay so much for records sold. At the end of every six months they figure out how many records are sold and presumably they pay you. Six thousand bucks or so is what they pay so it's a straight royalty fee." Along with creating a stable financial resource for a specified period of time this deal also helped to routinize the company's work again. The commitment to release three records a year meant that Theresa could return, at least in the short term, to a more predictable schedule of production.

These strategies were pursued in combination with each other, with the dominant one depending on the internal circumstances of the company and the external environment in which it operated. For instance, securing the European licensing deal reduced but did not eliminate the pressure to pursue more commercially oriented projects. These short-term solutions and strategies helped Theresa through difficulties that had their origins in the large environment.

FIVE

SOCIAL ORGANIZATION AND SOCIAL RELATIONSHIPS

Business-wise it makes sense to hire people that you don't know. But the trouble is that the business is in my home and that's difficult. I mean I don't want people that you don't have any feelings about walking around in your house.

Kazuko

For jazz critic Gary Giddins the most memorable jazz independents from the 1950s and 1960s embody "some aspect of the music so completely that we can't think of certain eras in jazz without invoking their names. They had a point of view and a style" (Giddins 1986: 68). In addition they maintained unique social organizations and relationships. Orrin Keepnews, a large bearded man who loved to talk about jazz, was an owner of one of the independents to which Giddins refers. You need only mention Thelonious Monk or Cannonball Adderley and Keepnews would respond with the enthusiasm gained from thirty years as a record executive and producer with Riverside Records and Fantasy Records. (In addition to Adderley and Monk, Keepnews has produced important recordings with Bill Evans, Wes Montgomery, Johnny Griffin, and Philly Joe Jones.) Keepnews believed that the distinctive style and organization at these companies were also partly a product of the entrepreneurs (mostly men) who ran independent labels and defined their direction and style. He referred to their aesthetic and organizational influence as the "cult of personality."

Keepnews fondly recalled that this early generation of independent company heads were men with distinctive personalities. "You just cannot write any kind of effective story of jazz history," he told me, "without recognizing just how heavily the individual personalities of a great many different musicians impacted the situation. In the same way, the extremely different personalities of a number of entrepreneurs and producers and exploiters and nonexploiters who were involved obviously had a lot to do with it" (Keepnews 1986). Along with Keepnews at Riverside, this early generation included Lester Koening at Contemporary Records, Alfred Lion and Frank Wolf at Blue Note, Bob Thiele at Impulse!, Bob Weinstock at Prestige, and Neshui Ertegun at Atlantic. During this period (and later) many artists, especially black musicians, also established their own independent labels. Among the lesser-known but significant attempts were Charles Mingus' and Max Roach's collaboration with Debut Records, Dizzy Gillespie's Dee Cee Records, Woody Herman's Mars Records, Lennie Tristano's Jazz Records, and Duke Ellington's Mercer label (Priestley 1982: 46). In the late 1960s pianist Stanley Cowell and trumpeter Charles Tolliver formed the Strata-East label; singer Betty Carter and composer Sun Ra have also maintained their own labels.

An important element in the pattern of ownership described by Keepnews is the fact that all the major owners of independent recording companies were white males. Indeed, it was the persistent pattern of exploitation and paternalism by white-owned recording companies (both majors and independents) that contributed to the distrust and suspicions of black popular and jazz musicians alike. Tales of musicians swindled out of royalties and composing credits by white executives and record company owners are legion in the recording industry. This pattern of exploitation and paternalism has partially fueled attempts by black musicians and entrepreneurs to own and control the terms of their music making. In this historical context the social relationships at independent recording companies described by Keepnews are particularly important. These experiences sharpen the significance of the social relationships and the quality of the interactions and participation that occur at independents.

Frith correctly cautions against celebrating entrepreneurs, but Keepnews' comments are instructive because they emphasize the significance of individual personalities in the independent experience:

> I'm not neither so naive nor immodest as to think that I did not have an effect on the period. I happen to believe in the importance of the conduit, the catalyst, the role that I filled. It's an important role. I think that sometimes maybe after all these years, I do get immodestly close to feeling that it is a creative role too. I think one other effect of the personality difference and the different ways of doing business and dealing with art that so many people had, it obviously had to affect the relationships between them and the musicians—those were partly financial, partly creative, and partly personal relationships and nobody really every stopped while it was going on to do much of a job of singling out the differences.

I don't want to overdo the "cult of personality" but, without exception, you look at the independent jazz scene and you see companies that are so small that they are virtually one or two-man operations. It's not just a matter of saying they were— we were virtually entire companies encased in one body and therefore the nature of that personality had an inordinate amount to do with it and that's the reason for that relationship. (Keepnews 1986)

One special quality of the independent experience for Keepnews was the close social relations he developed with musicians:

I had just a lot closer personal involvement with the musicians. It was almost like a team spirit thing, a sense of "this is our label." The way in which musicians who were working for Riverside would recommend talented musicians, and I know that there was a feeling, you know, guys playing for union scale on other guys' dates despite the fact that they were themselves stars. It was an expression of an attitude that belonged to that period and is among the things that cannot be recreated. (Keepnews 1986)

Keepnews identified some of the distinctive features that continue to define independents and the cultural space in which they operate. These experiences and relationships can be seen in more distinctly social and sociological terms rather than in terms of individual and personal characteristics. In fact the independent jazz company in the 1950s and 1960s was influenced by the organization of the entertainment industry (costs had not escalated and the business was not so big) and the fact that the dominant musical style of the period, bebop, was organized around an identifiable and cohesive jazz community based largely, though not exclusively, in New York. This community was small and composed of specific labels, clubs, audiences, critics, and musicians who shared a sense of community (Gillespie 1979). Changes in the size, costs, and structure of the recording industry and the erosion of the social and cultural circumstances that defined this earlier period have made it considerably more difficult to sustain the kind of social and cultural relationships that nourished this earlier generation of independent companies. Keepnews claimed that elements from this earlier period remained, but in greatly modified form.

Keepnews' current label, Landmark Records, is a case in point. "Landmark, as far as I am concerned, is by design about as close as one could hope to come to the pattern. It's by no means identical with it. It would be preposterous to try to be identical with what went on in the fifties, but it's an attempt to be a latter day equivalent of that. For example, it is virtually a one-man operation" (Keepnews 1986). Keepnews continued to see himself and his company in the mold of the old independent entrepreneur who shaped the direction of the company to his own vision. With Landmark he maintained artistic autonomy and organizational flexibility:

What I want from this company is for it to be able to maintain itself. Pay me a living wage and let me do the things I enjoy. I don't want it to be a company that will do nicely by hiring ten employees. I want it to have a certain shape and structure. Now that's severely influenced by what I have found to be healthy and artistically effective in the past. I've got an existing reputation, I've got a style, I've got a way of doing things and I just want to keep doing it that way. I'm probably inordinately or excessively proud of the fact that I'm doing this in my own special individual way. (Keepnews 1986)

I believe that Theresa Records also illustrates the extent to which the social relations and circumstances described by Keepnews remain, in modified form, a part of the independent experience. It is important to consider Theresa's social relations precisely because the company did not enjoy the benefits of access to major staff, promotion, and distribution of a company like Fantasy Records. Theresa's organization was not shielded from the structural turbulence but rather expressed the impact of that turbulence.

Especially relevant to Theresa's particular expression of social organization were the shifts in the physical location of the company and changes in the company personnel. In the course of my five-year contact with them, Theresa operated from three different locations and experienced several changes in personnel. The major portion of my interactions and observations with Kazuko, Allen, and Paul occurred when they operated the company from Kazuko's home. It was this period, as we've seen, when the company first achieved national recognition. It was also in this period that it released many of the major titles in its current catalogue.

Social Organization and Social Relations at Theresa

Between 1979 and 1983 the major administrative and management duties at Theresa were divided among Kazuko, Paul, and Allen. Kazuko handled the promotion, bookings for musicians, and the accounting. She also coordinated Theresa's album projects, which meant that she managed the various stages in the creation, assembly, and promotion of the record. She regularly developed and placed advertisements and other promotional materials required to ensure maximum exposure for the records.

Although much of Paul's work was part time during this period, he was nevertheless a central player in the life of the company. His major responsibility consisted of developing and maintaining Theresa's relationship with its network of distributors. He also coordinated inventory and tracked sales. Most importantly, Paul had "big ears." His musical judgments and aesthetic contributions were major and he was usually central to editing and mixing sessions. The rhythm of Paul's work was organized in intense spurts of activity that took place immediately before and after a record's release. This irregular rhythm often meant periods of hectic, often intense activity followed by relatively long periods of inactivity. During these less demanding periods, Paul concentrated on his own musical projects.

Allen's responsibility during this period consisted of activities associated with being executive producer. As co-owner of Theresa, Allen assumed (and shared with Kazuko) responsibility for major financial and aesthetic decisions. In the company's formative years and for a considerable period thereafter, Allen made all the major decisions. With Theresa's increased visibility both Paul and Kazuko became more central in major decisions.

Although I have described these activities according to a clear division of labor, in the day-to-day life of the company the activities were shared by everyone as need and their availability permitted. I became aware of this situation when Kazuko explained why she always seemed to take so much responsibility for various tasks. Kazuko used her relationship with Paul to explain why things seemed consistently to shake out this way. "I've discovered that he [Paul] is not good with arithmetic. I mean he's capable of doing it [inventory], but his main interest in music. So what happens is that he'll be going over someone's statement and then I'm sure he'll start thinking about his own music and his mind wanders off and he'll make a huge error" (Kazuko 1981). This crucial realization resulted in an adjustment in Paul's responsibilities: "We found out that Paul is an excellent editor of musicians. When he goes into the studio, he can chop out a whole section and condense a whole piece to a half. . . .So those are the areas where he's best suited because he loves it. He finds it challenging and creative" (Kazuko 1981). This simple, but significant, adjustment was possible because of the small size of the company and the informal nature of the group process. So even though Kazuko's and Allen's main responsibilities were managerial and administrative, they also did everything, including serving as producers, stage hands, and road managers.[1] This distribution of responsibility is, in fact, consistent with the relationships and organization alluded to by Keepnews and identified by Rothschild-Whitt in studies of small collectivist-based organizations (1979). In contrast to formal bureaucracies she found these small organizations structured informally according to shared responsibility.

The interactions at Theresa were rooted in the principles of friendship, shared responsibility, and mutual trust, and they developed from the close personal relationships among all the members of the company. Indeed, Theresa operated on the basis of the kind of one-on-one relationships described earlier by Keepnews. Allen and Kazuko were, for instance, close personal friends as well as business partners. (As I noted in Chapter Three, Kazuko became a partner in the company because of her friendship with Allen.) Similarly, Paul joined the company as a result of his and Allen's previous musical association in the One Mind Experience.[2]

As they evolved, these friendships formed the social basis for the identity and organization of Theresa (Rothschild-Whitt 1979; Selznick 1949). They expressed a sense of community "where relations are holistic, personal, and [of] value in themselves" (Rothschild-Whitt 1979). This is the sense of community that Keepnews so valued from his Riverside experiences. In fact I think that the company's small size and the close friendships among the members helped Kazuko and her colleagues approximate, in a modified form, the experiences of the earlier generation of jazz independents.

This social organization both materially and ideologically provided the company with a sense of cohesion, direction, identity, and purpose and helped shape its products, define the organization of work within the company, and contribute to its public identity. In my field notes I noted that there was a specific organizational character during my initial visit to a mixing session for Rejoice (TR112/1139):

Kazuko and Allen see the company as a small company that has managed to maintain its level of integrity and commitment to the pursuit of the music that they believe in. This has worked out with them attracting artists with whom they share particular kinds of common ground musically, commercially,

and philosophically. . . . Several artists with the company
exude what I would call a kind of spirituality, a kind of self-
conscious identification and representation of themselves and
their work as spiritual.

My use of the vague notion of "spirituality" says something about the difficulty of precisely defining the quality of
the members' particular social relationships. Sometime later
Kazuko described the basis of these interactions in terms of
personal compatibility: "You could have somebody who's
terrific, . . . the music might be okay, we might like it, but
the personality, if the feeling from the people is not right,
then we don't want to do it either. I guess it narrows it down
[to] musical direction and the spirituality of the people producing the music. We really don't want to deal with a lot of
nasty people (Kazuko 1981). Given the material circumstances
of the company (e.g., its size and its location in her home)
these kinds of social relations made sense. They provided
Kazuko with the social resources necessary to organize the
work while providing some way of managing the potential
social and personal uncertainties she routinely encountered.

In the following excerpt from an early interview, Kazuko
described these relationships in terms of the record company
as a family. Her comments also illustrate the depth of Theresa's commitment to the social relations and why they were
so central.

Q: Have you had any thoughts of bringing anyone else into
the company?
Kazuko: I would like to find someone, but it's hard to find
somebody. I guess I'm getting kinda pessimistic about finding

anybody who's reliable and who has the kinds of skills that we want.

Q: Perhaps you may not have to rely so much on the family conception?

Kazuko: It might make more sense. I mean the family, as far as the business is concerned, . . . might be a mistake. For example, when Pharoah came out here he was gonna have a local drummer. Todd Barkan called and said, "Look, this is ridiculous, paying him so much money. We should have at least some other person from out of town." So we talked Pharoah into getting Idris to come out.

Well what happened then was that Idris stayed at Allen's house. We picked him up at the airport, we took him to the gig every night, and we took him to the airport when he left. It [meant] getting up at five in the morning and that kind of thing. Afterward I said, "Wait a minute, the booking agent, if anybody, should be taking care of that, right?" I mean she's the one making the commission, we're not. But because of this family feeling about Idris we take care of him. In terms of business, I mean, business people wouldn't do that, right? But you know what happened is that Idris came over here Sunday and cooked gumbo. I have this tape that says Idris's gumbo and he's telling how to make gumbo.

Q: So the family thing is getting a lot more inefficient?

Kazuko: Well it take a lot of tolls. I don't know about the inefficiency, yeah inefficiency. I think that it might be a good idea to hire people. Businesswise it makes sense to hire people that you don't know. But the trouble is that the business is in my home and that's difficult. I mean I don't want people that you don't have any feelings about walking around in your house [laughter]. (Kazuko 1980)

It seems to me that two issues are raised here. First, music occupied a central place in the lives of Allen and Kazuko and so a "music first" attitude was constantly expressed by everyone. Second, the location of the company, at this point, in Kazuko's home required a form of social organization that ensured that people were loyal and trustworthy and could get along. As Kazuko noted, while it perhaps showed poor business judgment, she still did not want to open her home to complete strangers.

This approach to social relations also defined the aesthetic work in the company. Not only was this sense of cohesion important to getting records out and maintaining the routine affairs of the company, but it was also important in the relationship between Allen and Kazuko and the musicians. After a series of bad experiences with record companies Pharoah, for example, appreciated the combination of personal trust and aesthetic space that he found at Theresa:

> Theresa helped out with the business. They let me do basically what I wanted to do. That's why I stuck with Doc [Allen]. He really trusts my judgment. I want to see them make some money. I want to see them do well. They have treated me with respect in every way—warmth, friendliness, trust. (Pharoah 1986).

George Coleman was also attracted to the quality of social relations at Theresa. This is how Kazuko described the formation of Theresa's relationship with him:

> It just happens. It just falls into our laps. You know, like George Coleman says, "I'd like to do a recording" and we say, Yeah, that would be great. We didn't search him out. He talked about he liked the company and he liked what we

were doing and he just liked the notions and he wanted to do a record with us. . . . He hadn't recorded with an American company in I don't know how long. He said he didn't trust them. (Kazuko 1986)

These informal relationships also helped establish the framework for how recording projects developed. The importance of trust, understanding, and freedom in the relationship between Allen and Pharoah is also very much in evidence in the following account by Allen of the evolution of *Shukuru* (TR121):

It was just a kind of evolving thing. I think the first thing that happened was—we were talking about doing something [an album]. It [the idea for the recording session] took off after we heard what the synthesizer could do and the fact that it could do strings and voices. [Pharoah] always wanted to do that anyway. It really evolved that way. It had a loose beginning and developed as it went along. (Allen 1986)

In these examples, the mark of Theresa's social organization and social relationships is evident. It was expressed in Pharoah's and George's attraction to the company because of their trust and good feelings for Allen and Kazuko. It was also expressed in the flexibility available for Pharoah's searching and unorthodox planning approach to *Shukuru*. These qualities express the organizational freedom and closeness that I first detected early in my observations. They are, I think, contemporary approximations of qualities that defined social relationships at jazz independents in the 1950s and 1960s.

Problems and Tensions of Social Relations at Theresa

The flip size of viewing Theresa Records as an open and trusting environment involved, for Allen and Kazuko, the costs of managing these close interpersonal relationships in such a highly charged setting. Indeed, if Theresa's social organization and relationships contributed to the creation of a trusting and open environment, it sometimes came at significant social and personal cost. For Kazuko the personal and emotional costs were, at times, especially heavy:

> Q: We talked a little about the division of labor in the company by sex. Do you have any thoughts about it?
>
> Kazuko: Well, I think it's typical. I mean, what I'm doing is typically a woman's role in the family, right? There's your mother who picks up after you and makes sure everything is done. . . . I feel like I take on that primary responsibility of making sure everything is done in the best possible way, you know, the completion of tasks. Men are great initiators, that's their tradition.
>
> Q: We've talked a lot about "family" and you have an understanding of what it means. You started to approach it by talking about the mother's role. Is it expressed in other ways?
>
> Kazuko: Well I don't always feel like I'm the mother. Very often I think it's like the brother and sister, that concept of the family, especially with artists. I mean occasionally I don't feel motherly toward the artists, but I sometimes feel the frustration and annoyance that mothers feel toward their children.

When I'm dealing with someone like Joe, sometimes he'll call me five times a day. For the last nine or ten months he's been charging telephone bills to our phone and I have to tell him "don't do it" and in fact I tell the telephone company, "I don't know who's doing it but he's unauthorized." I tell Joe, "Look, it takes too much of my time. I have to call the phone company twice a month at least. We have to go over calculations and it takes up a lot of my time and I don't want to do it so please don't charge calls to my number." In that way I feel that he makes me act like a mother toward him. I mean, it's disciplinary and I resent that. I mean, I don't want to be that way.

Q: Is the relationship that you've described with Joe typical of your relationship with other musicians?

Kazuko: No, definitely not. But I think that it's a difficult world for them. If they find that they can do that, then they'll try. There is the general feeling that when I'm in a bind, my family, the record company, will help me out. That is a problem and the way I see it is that I'd like to keep this family feeling, but without this thing of dependency. We should all be able to stand alone but work together. Maybe that isn't family. Maybe everybody has to do his part. That's the way I try to run my own family. (Kazuko 1980)

Kazuko experienced a number of these problems directly and took responsibility for addressing them in part because she was a major partner in the company, but also and importantly because the company was, at this point, located in her home. For both these reasons a lot of the culture and identity Theresa took reflected Kazuko's distinct vision. Occasionally Kazuko's emotional involvement got especially intense in her relationship with Pharoah. His shy manner and sometimes indirect, intuitive style of communication often made for misunderstandings and frustrations. This frustration led Kazuko, in retrospect, to note:

> If we want to keep operating we can't do too many foolish things. For example, like this emotional investment in Pharoah. You think that he wants to do something and so you start putting out a lot of energy toward it and he says, "Oh, I don't think I'll do it." It's sort of disappointing . . . [here the sentence trailed off and her laughter seemed to mask her frustration and disappointment]. So if you try to second guess him we're going to be in trouble because he's going to want something different. (Kazuko 1986).

These informal relations, nurtured as they were in Kazuko's home, exposed Theresa's vulnerabilities and created dependencies. The social relationships also presented Kazuko and Allen with problems in the application of organizational sanctions, the maintenance of (minimal levels of) efficiency, and financial abuse by musicians who were not loyal to the company.

Consider, for instance, the application of organizational sanctions to employees and its impact on the operation and morale of the company. Theresa regularly subcontracted the preparation of promotional materials, liner notes, photography, and the design of record jackets. Artists usually worked on their own according to a production schedule established by them and Kazuko. When a project (photograph, liner comments, jacket layout) was completed, the artist met with Kazuko, Allen, office personnel, and the musicians involved to review the work. Because it was a contractual arrangement, it was imperative that artists meet deadlines and maintain contacts with Kazuko to keep her aware of the various projects.

This was the social context in which Dan, Theresa's major graphic artist, worked. He joined them because a previous artist left in the middle of the project. Although Dan was Theresa's principal graphic artist, he did not work for them exclusively or full time. This meant that he was very often not around (or in touch with Kazuko) on a routine basis. Nonetheless, Dan was regarded as a member of the company.

Prior to Dan's arrival Theresa's record jackets were limited in their visual appeal. Covers were typically presented with few colors, standard publicity photographs, limited graphics, and sparse liner notes. With Dan's arrival, Theresa's album packages became more colorful, imaginative, and visually interesting. With *Journey to the One* (TR108/109) and *Rejoice* (TR112/113) double jackets with fold-out format replaced the conventional one-piece jacket. Conventional publicity photographs of musicians were replaced with candid shots while cover notes were written by noted critics and commentators. These changes reflect the fact that Theresa had established a public identity and had released material by internationally recognized artists.

Dan also shared some of that special spirituality that defined Theresa. He, for instance, often incorporated the musicians' ideas into the visual presentation of their music; Theresa's second album cover with Pharoah, for example, centered on one of his favorite personal possessions, a strip of African kinte cloth. Although by no means unique to small companies, the active involvement of musicians in this phase of the production process was yet another expression of the social relations found at small independents.[3]

On at least two separate projects, however, Dan was unusually late completing the covers. In one case, because of his free-lance activities, he was also unavailable for consultation on the progress of the covers at important points in the production schedule. At the meeting that was finally scheduled Dan presented mockups of the covers (which by this point were behind schedule), which were at different stages of development and in need of considerable work before their release date. Allen and Kazuko found themselves in a precarious position. Disappointed and displeased with Dan's slow progress and irresponsible attitude, they were also far too committed to the projects to start over with a new artist. They also liked Dan's work and continued to regard him an integral part of the company. Consequently, they were cautious but firm in communicating their displeasure and disappointment. Kazuko was critical but encouraging; Allen was more concerned with completing the projects and meeting the scheduled deadline. As might be expected the projects were completed well after their scheduled (and publicly announced) release dates. Shortly after this episode Dan's formal relationship with Theresa ended. For Kazuko it was not so much the level or quality of Dan's work that posed problems, but the way in which he handled his responsibilities.

In this situation the costs of informal social organization and primary-based relationships were inefficiency, production delays, and the inability to sanction Dan. The size and scale of the company required that the distribution and coordination of resources be done in a systematic fashion. Because resources were limited and the company was small, Dan's behavior disrupted production and revealed the company's limitations in managing disruptions. Because it was rooted in the very structure of the company this pattern was repeated again and again.

Problems generated by social relations and organization also stemmed from the tensions between the personal needs of company members and the organization's ability to respond to these needs. Because of the company's size, organization, and dependence on the loyalty and commitment of the members, these tensions constantly reverberated throughout the company. What follows is Kazuko's description of the circumstances surrounding the termination of Theresa's relationship with one member who worked with Paul in distribution and also functioned as the general office manager. "She told me that some days she can't deal with the world. She's afraid that if she opens her mouth and makes a phone call, she can't make it because somehow the world can get to her. She gets frightened, so she claims, and stays at home and works on art until she feels better" (Kazuko 1981). In a longer exchange Kazuko identified the company's social relations and style of organization as a possible cause for this situation and for how they handled it:

> *Kazuko:* Because you're not rigid people assume that you're sloppy and there's a big difference between flexibility and sloppiness. I'm sure that she thought that, "well, I don't feel well and if I don't come in that'll be okay because she [Kazuko] understands." But it's not okay! I still have to get this work done, and if she doesn't come that means that I have to do

it. And when she said that she was going to come in one day
and didn't, I had to go running around to the stripper and the
color separator and do all of the stuff that she was supposed
to do for me. Which means that I couldn't count records. She
didn't seem to understand that. To her because I'm an understanding person I would say "Oh, that's all right, you
know, just go take care of yourself." Which I'd love to say,
but there's also work that has to be done.

Q: How do you sanction members of the company when
they fail to do what you want?

Kazuko: With [her] I talk to her—"Look, I need these things
to be done and if you can't do them, then we have to get
somebody who can. It's up to you. Either do them or we get
somebody else to do them."

Q: It seems important that you maintain the familial character even if you have to part company.

Kazuko: I don't think that if you part company that you
have to be hostile. The reason for the parting should be made
clear and there doesn't have to be any nastiness. It's just that
"you couldn't do this for us therefore we can't work with
you." If a person is willing to accept that, there should be no
animosity. I guess I don't like unpleasantness. I guess it's
important to me.

Q: Does this extend to the relationship with musicians as
well?

Kazuko: I think that it's become more evident to Allen that
the best way to do it is to be very straight with people. I think
his method of dealing with things on the past has been neglect.
I mean if he didn't want to say no he would just say, "Well,
don't tell them I'm in," you know [laughing], just put people
off. But he's realizing that hurts people and that it's best to
just tell them no and why not and just be very straight with
people. And that's what I've done with [the office manager].

That's why the last night she came to get her final check, she gave both of us a big hug and said, "I'll keep in touch."

Q: That's important to you?

Kazuko: It's important to me, yeah, because I like her. I have no objections to her as a person and she seemed to understand that. I hate that things get confused, business, people, relationships. I don't want people to think I fired them because I didn't like them, 'cause that would be a misconception. I should be able to tell a person, "Look your work is great but I can't stand having you around." In other kinds of settings, people say you don't have to like people you work with, but in this case, it's very important that you like them.

Q: Because you're around them?

Kazuko: Oh! And they're making coffee in your kitchen! (Kazuko 1981)

Even where Kazuko found it impossible to maintain a consistent work relationship (as with the office manager) she continued to emphasize the personal dimension of their relationship. This emphasis on the social relationships expressed the essence of Theresa's organizational character.

As one might guess, word of Allen and Kazuko's commitment to the music and their sensitivity to musicians got around among musicians. As a consequence their public identity and reputation was sometimes a source of problems, especially in their relationship to musicians more peripheral to the company. In the music business it is common to use session and studio musicians as a supporting cast for a featured artist on a recording session or live performance (Faulkner 1971; Peterson and White 1979). For Kazuko, Allen, and Paul this meant prolonged contact with musicians and others who did not necessarily share their general identity and ideology. One particularly unpleasant situation with a musician occurred because Allen and Kazuko lacked a systematic means of coordinating and allocating their resources.

Q: Paul, you once mentioned the case of a musician who charged you a large sum of money for a studio session.

Kazuko: Yea, that was the rip off that we had. . . .

Paul:[A] conga player. I wasn't there. We didn't have a budget set up for the percussionist.

Kazuko: It was clearly a rip off because he had been there the day before and he was paid union [the standard fee established by the musician's union] and he was asked to come back the next day and do something else and that's when he insisted on two thousand dollars.

Paul: That's when had we been clear about what we could afford for each record, it would have been easier for us to say, "Of course not."

Kazuko: Oh no! Allen knew he was being ripped off because if you pay him "x" for day one you pay him "x" for day two.

Paul: I mean it was clear, very clear, that he [the musician] had a very strong background. . . . We're getting used to working with it now.[4] (Allen, Kazuko, Paul 1981)

Kazuko (and Paul) also saw this experience in terms of Theresa's organizational style and the company's somewhat naive reliance on personal social relationships to regulate its formal business negotiations: "I guess we went under the assumption that people would treat you fairly if you treated them fairly. Apparently that's not the case. So we have to know what the guidelines are. It's also our fault for not being businesslike. I think people misunderstand that as meaning you're flaky. If you don't give a hard line about business, then people will think, 'Well, they're loose and it doesn't matter.'"

Aware of the need for organizational modifications to avoid future exploitation, Kazuko took this experience to heart. Notice her attempt to hold onto the company's organizational style even as she pondered how to protect themselves:

> I've said to Pharoah, "Look, I want you to give us input, especially on your records. I'd like for you to tell us how much we should offer to pay musicians." And I tell him, "Allen thinks it should be this much," and he says, "No, no, no. That's too much. You shouldn't pay them that much. . . . Oh no, that's too much. That's too steep." What it does is give the musicians the wrong attitude about the company. You know they think that you've got lots of money and if you offer them too much, then they don't feel the urgency to help themselves. To help sell records themselves and realize that everybody's working for the same end. If you give them a lot of money they think, "Well, they can afford it. We don't have to do anything, we can just go along for the ride." (Kazuko 1981)

In spite of this negative experience Kazuko also reminded me of the circumstances that often led to antagonistic relationships between musicians and record companies. She continued to emphasize the importance of Theresa's social relationships and the ideological values that guided them:

> We should probably talk more about money from the start instead of assuming that everyone's gonna be reasonable. One of the things that I think you have to remember is that mu-

sicians have been ripped off for a long time. They're accustomed to being ripped off by so-called record companies and so when they see an opportunity that they can perhaps get paid for their past injustices, they take it. (Kazuko 1981)

By 1986, with the wisdom of ten years and the effects of these and similar experiences still fresh in their memories, both Allen and Kazuko seemed somewhat more inclined toward more explicit organizational and financial rules. First, Kazuko's observations:

I think we made mistakes with some of the earlier ones [projects]. Silly things like not having a clear agreement with the musicians before we started to record and then finding out that they wanted more than we thought they did. That kind of thing. So I remind Allen to make it absolutely clear before they start what we can afford. Because he tends to just let it all float by and then realizes that when he's asked for more money that he didn't make it clear. (Kazuko 1986)

Allen's reflections also resonate with wisdom gained from time, distance, and experience:

I'm trying to get my business stuff more straightened out—standard contracts and stuff like that. We did contracts initially and a lot of it sort of disappeared. Because we're not making any money we haven't gotten to the break-even point very often so a lot of it is academic. [But] I just wanna get it straightened out. I realize that it's not a good idea. You really need things spelled out because things might happen. (Allen 1986)

The situations with the graphic artist, the office manager,

and the musicians all suggest that the organization of Theresa according to informal social relations created problems that were continually felt in all aspects of the operation, especially in the personal lives of Allen and Kazuko. The absence of organizational boundaries and clear rules threatened the stability of the company. These and similar situations produced stresses and disruptions that directly affected the ability of Allen, Kazuko, and Paul to manage their work. In the short term they responded to these stresses by attempting to increase organizational efficiency while maintaining the informal and personal basis of the social relationships. They did this by reducing the number of new projects while they explored a more systematic way to allocate resources. Paul's comments reflect this strategy:

> We're aware now of how much we spend on recordings. I mean that two thousand dollars—if that had been cut down to two hundred, we would have been able to make that much of a profit and be able to kick so much back to the musicians. I mean we're starting to see (and be able to put things into perspective) how important a little decision like that is in the very beginning of the life of the record company and the artist. This way we can make it; otherwise we're gonna be digging our hole. (Paul 1981)

In 1983, Allen and Kazuko moved to offices in downtown Albany. With this move the label continued to mature and sharpen its public identity, and it continued to release significant records, but its financial and organizational situation remained unstable. After two years, escalating production costs, problems with distribution and payment, and internal staff changes forced them to move the company to Allen's house.

The company took on a slightly different resonance with the move to Allen's place. This is not all that suprising since it involved a new location and new major players. Where Kazuko's influence on the organization was dominant in the period when the company operated out of her house, by the time of their move to Allen's and my return to follow up the company's development, she was less visible and active in day-to-day operations. Kazuko assumed a more subdued role because she returned, full time, to her professional research career. The move produced a discernible change in the organization, work, and division of labor in the company. With the move to his place, Allen became the primary force in the operation and direction of the company.

In 1986, from the garage office at his house, Allen recalled the circumstances that led to this last round of organizational adjustments: "It's just too damned expensive. We were paying seven hundred bucks a month rent [for the office space]. When Beth [the last staff employee] left it was just Kazuko and I and my son. We decided to consolidate and save our money. Actually it [the office] was nice. It was nice to have an office. It was easier. It would become difficult again if we hired more than just our family." In the long term, the problems of organizational efficiency coalesced with many of the financial problems already described in Chapter Four. In response to the collective weight of these organizational and financial tensions Allen and Kazuko were forced to operate with a minimum production schedule and reduce the staff. The aim of both these short- and long-term strategies was to increase organizational efficiency and retain the special organizational character that defined the company.

The move of the company to a new office temporarily altered the immediate structural circumstances that produced Theresa's particular organization and social relations. This new setting eased the pressures and conflicts generated by the conjuncture of Kazuko's home, the informal social organization, small size, and the requirements for compatible social relations. In this location Kazuko and Allen could exercise a bit more flexibility about who could join the company and how they could function. This situation produced a more explicit move toward formalizing the social relationships.

At the same time Allen and Kazuko were still guided by the ideology and experiences from social relationships previously established at Kazuko's. This tension between a new organizational setting and the persistence of an old ideology that defined their social relations and aesthetic directions was exacerbated by various internal and external stresses that continued to plague the company. As Allen suggested, the move to the office resolved some of the immediate problems of privacy and the separation of Allen's and Kazuko's public and private lives. It was, at least structurally, possible to establish a more formal set of social relationships among various members of the company. The office was still expensive, however, and as the size of the staff continued to decline, the costs of maintaining it became increasingly prohibitive since the cutback in production had resulted in reduced revenues.

Once again the company became an extremely lean operation and was forced to move. Although this time they maintained elements of the older ideology, they also faced a different set of social and structural circumstances (e.g., the licensing deal from Europe, a scaled-downed production schedule, new distributors). This meant that, at least for the short term, the immediate problems of organization and social relationships abated.

Theresa's Spirituality: A Final Note

Theresa Records was more than a collection of roles held together by formally prescribed principles. The location of the company, the personalities and tastes of Allen, Kazuko, Paul, and Pharoah as well as their economic situation played a central role in shaping the members' work, their products, and the selection of potential musicians and members.

The kind of organizational strategies a firm adopts is related to the nature of its external environment (e.g., the degree of market competition): the "greater the turbulence of the relevant environment, the less the formal structure of the subsystem and the greater the entrepreneurship" (Peterson and Berger 1971). The more predictable and stable the social environment, the more record companies rely on bureaucratic modes of organization and collaboration. Furthermore, as Theresa's situation suggests, the turbulence of the internal environment also influences the organizational strategies adopted by firms.

Cultural organizations strive for predictability and innovation at the same time that they attempt to manage the inherent turbulence in the popular music environment (DiMaggio 1977). The need for predictability and innovation forces all manufacturers of popular music, regardless of size, into a dilemma: the desire to control their markets and the constant need for product innovation. The extent to which these twin demands are met and effectively managed determines whether the general market turbulence that firms face will be eliminated or minimized or whether it will continue unabated. To the extent that cultural organizations are not able to meet and effectively respond to these demands for control, then stylistic innovation, product diversity, and competition in the industry will likely result (DiMaggio 1977).

At large major companies, formal bureaucratic organization minimizes the disruptions and frustrations created by the need for predictability and innovation. Manufacturing processes, which are more adaptable to routinization (e.g., manufacture, sales, promotion, distribution), are organized into a formal bureaucracy. The less predictable creative activities are isolated and organized on the basis of organizational flexibility and collaboration. In such an arrangement there is little tolerance for internal disruption such as that found at Theresa, and where it does occur, it is isolated and does not directly affect the total organization. At these firms there is collaboration and coordination between various departments, but it is always with the aim of minimizing internal disruption and maximizing organizational efficiency.

Companies like Theresa do not have the organizational resources necessary to manage the environmental turbulence that they face in the same way as major firms. Because informal social relationships were so central to Theresa's work and identity, bureaucratic approaches would not work. Initially, the operation of the company from Kazuko's home established the terms of Theresa's social organization, social relations, and identity. That the record company was in Kazuko's home had much to do with who became a member of the company. It was important that those working in the organization got along and that they shared the implicit spirit and good will that they found there. So important was this criterion that capable musicians were sometimes turned away or found wanting if they could not fit into this social context.

Obviously it is possible for a company to remain independent in terms of its identity, ideology, and social relations and yet remain a bureaucratically structured organization. In many cases independent companies deliberately organize themselves according to bureaucratic principles simply because they view such an arrangement as the most efficient way to handle the various organizational demands they face. In still others formal organization nominally exists, perhaps to satisfy legal requirements, but in practice the companies carry out their day-to-day operations according to more informal and less structured principles.[5]

As I show in the next chapter, in the context of this set of organizational relationships Allen, Kazuko, Paul, and the musicians constructed an ideological and aesthetic vision of themselves and the company. Although this ideology was not always explicit, it was shared by Kazuko, Paul, and Allen, the musicians, and their audiences. The feelings and meanings that Kazuko called "spirituality" guided their work, defined their music, and provided a public identity.

SIX

PRODUCING JAZZ: THE SIGNIFICANCE OF THERESA RECORDS

I could push Joe's album all day because it says something to people that I would like passed. . . . It does something to me and I think it would do a similar thing to other people.

Paul

Max Horkheimer and Theodor Adorno were among the earliest observers to appreciate the commodity character of popular culture.[1] They observed, "No object has any inherent value; it is only valuable . . . to the extent that it can be exchanged. The use value of art, its mode of being is treated like a fetish, the work's social rating . . . becoming its use value—the only quality which is enjoyed" (9172: 158). Since profit is the driving motivation in the recording industry, the uses of popular music for many cultural producers have little to do with its intrinsic meaning. This results in a situation where music "no longer has any qualitative value in itself, but insofar as it can be used, the various forms of activity lose their imminent intrinsic satisfaction as activity and become means to an end" (Jameson 1979: 131).

The rise of the commodity character of popular culture is related to the industrial and economic circumstances of its production and consumption. Thus to the extent that all symbolic culture is produced for profit in an industrialized system of production, it will bear the stamp of the commodity form and the conditions of its production (Jameson 1979). In this situation the commercial value of popular music prevails as the dominant motivation of producers (Frith 1981). They key to this commercial system of production is the market, which "denotes the audience as it is identified and conceptualized by financial decision-makers within a popular culture industry. When such people say there is no market for a particular cultural work, or that the market won't accept it, they mean that, in their opinion, not enough of a profit can be realized to justify the production, distribution, and promotion of the item" (Peterson 1982: 146).

Todd Gitlin has cogently described the process by which this commercial production system, based on the organization of the market, also forms a basis for the social meaning at the level of consumption:

> In advanced capitalist societies, popular culture is the meeting ground for two linked (through not identical) social processes. (1) The culture industry *produces its goods, tailoring them to particular markets and organizing their content so that they are packaged to be compatible with the dominant values and dominant discourse.* And (2) by consuming clumps of these cultural goods *distinct social groups help position themselves in the society and work toward defining their status, their social identity. By enjoying a certain genre of music, film, television program, they take a large step toward recognizing themselves as a social entity. (1982: 3, my emphasis)*

Although dominant, this commercial view of popular music and its consumers is by no means the only one. From another angle, popular music also expresses the experiences and meanings of its users, which are separate from the intentions of its producers. These meanings may or may not correspond to those intended by the producers or those gatekeepers and support personnel who legitimate and sustain the dominant conceptions and definitions (Hall 1973; Hebdige 1979). Conditioned by their social location and experiences, people develop different, sometimes conflicting, and often contradictory meanings and uses for their music (Hebdige 1979; Willis 1978). These meanings and experiences very often lie outside and beyond the reach of major manufacturers.

Such experiences are illustrated by the cases of punk, reggae, and rap musics. The images and symbols articulated by these genres represent meanings and experiences that challenge or, at the very least, exist beyond the dominant racial and class arrangements. And yet even these alternative experiences are potentially absorbed into the cultural mainstream, where they are consumed by and incorporated into the meaning systems of different social groups, including the dominant groups (Gitlin 1982; Hebdige 1979; Toop 1984). Popular culture is always expressed as both economic commodity and an ensemble of cultural meanings, artifact and lived experience, industry product and cultural practice (Frith 1981; Gitlin 1982; Hall 1977; Hebdige 1979; Williams 1977; Willis 1978).

A small independent cultural producer like Theresa Records deliberately privileges the cultural significance of its music over the commercial significance. Indeed, the emphasis on cultural meanings is a distinguishing feature of Theresa. At the same time, even though Allen, Kazuko, and Paul regarded the cultural meanings of their work as predominant, they also recognized that they had to sell their records. Independents may be small, but they operate in capitalist environments, according to capitalists rules, and are capitalists nonetheless (Frith 1981).

The reality of the music industry is sufficiently complex that the activities of large majors cannot be equated only with the commodification of music (and the corruption of its meanings) and independents only with preserving its cultural significance. Frith's argument against this line of reasoning is persuasive, since popular music, regardless of where it is produced, always expresses both use value and exchange value. Meanings, moreover, are not necessarily and completely given by the intentions of producers and manufacturers. Rather they are constructed by audiences in interaction with the artifact and the experiences they bring to it.

The experiences at Theresa Records indicate the presence of these fractured and contradictory meanings; they were expressed in company discussions about the aesthetic appeal of fusion and the efficacy of releasing commercial music. Theresa's experiences also show that independent firms do privilege and express aesthetic impulses and social experiences of the kind described by Jameson. The central argument of this book is that these impulses are concretely expressed in Theresa's organization of work, its social relationships and forms of social collaboration, its public identity, and its music.

The Social Meaning of Music at Theresa

In *Profane Culture* Paul Willis shows how music, motorcycle, drugs, and social relationships of two subcultures—motorbike boys and hippies—provided members with identity and cohesion (1978). These objects contained and were themselves embedded in a complex set of social, political, and economic relationships that helped to shape the identities and meanings of the members of these subcultures. Like the profane objects in the subcultures Willis observed, Kazuko, Allen, and Paul regarded jazz as much more than a means to a financial end. Their enthusiasm sometimes bordered on zealousness.[2] Such commitment and enthusiasm is evident, for example, in a comment by Paul about one of Theresa's artists:

> I'm pushing Joe's album more than any album I've pushed. . . . I can appreciate what he's saying and I really appreciate his arranging talents on the thing. He busted his balls; . . . he did some great work and made it right. I'm a little bit more behind this one than I've been on any of the other records including many of the ones that I'm on. It makes a difference. I think that the sales people pick up on it. I could push Joe's album all day because its says something to people that I would like passed. . . . It does something to me and I think it would do a similar thing to other people (Paul 1981).

The intensity of this commitment to the music, more than anything else, motivated and helped Paul and his colleagues to make sense of their activity.

The significance of music in the personal and collective lives of Kazuko, Allen, and Paul was also at the heart of their collective definition of the company. Again an exchange between the three principal members of the company illustrates this point.

Allen: Music tries to make people feel better. At least people's [long pause] . . . you can call it spirituality. . . .

Paul: Positivity. . . .

Kazuko: . . . We should name the company "Elevation Records.". . .

Allen: . . . It's too bad that you can't do everything by trade. You play a gig, it's too bad somebody can't give you a room for a month. . . . The idea of contributing and getting something back on some kind of level that you contribute.

Paul: Or, a more straightforward trade, like you've made me feel good by playing music. Here's something that can make you feel good. I mean I hate nothing more than to go into a club and play my heart out and people really like it and then I have to go and fight with a club owner to see if he's gonna cover my gas money. Most people that we deal with are in it [the company] because they are selling the music that they really want to sell. (Allen, Kazuko, Paul 1981)

These observations might appear idealistic, even naive, yet they convey the importance of feelings about music and its place in people's lives. In spite of their enthusiasm Kazuko, Allen, and Paul nevertheless recognized the need to maintain financial stability. They regarded commercial success as a priority insofar as it provided the financial security necessary to stay in business.

This shared experience and definition of music provided Theresa with organizational and ideological cohesion and it helped shape its public identity as a respectable record company. In fact, one of the company's explicit aims was to share its special experience of the music with its audience. So central was this commitment (and the company's reputation) that the costs of allocating and mobilizing its resources often exceeded its financial means.

For instance, my field notes indicate that, in January 1981, Theresa paid to fly a Japanese koto player from Seattle to San Francisco especially for a concert where she performed with Pharoah on the opening tune for each of two sets. Pharoah's debut recording on Theresa had featured him on several selections with this koto player, and because of their musical compatibility, Pharoah wanted to feature her at the San Francisco concert. Allen, Kazuko, and Paul agreed with the idea especially in light of the success of the previous recorded collaboration.[3] In another example, Allen, reflecting on Theresa's early projects with Pharoah, revealed that he thought that the release of two double albums of Pharoah's material was a financial mistake. The problem lay in the fact that there was enough material available for four separate records, which, in the long run, certainly would have been more cost efficient.

The financial costs in the second example and the personal inconveniences endured in the first did not deter Theresa from their musical commitments. In both cases the importance of presenting music that expressed Theresa's sensibility and aesthetic commitment took priority over the financial and personal costs. This commitment to aesthetic integrity and stylistic direction, in the face of the constant need for financial stability, led to discussions about the uneasy tension within the company between aesthetics and commerce.

Tensions Between Aesthetics and Commerce

Like their organization and social relations, Theresa's aesthetic commitments were also somewhat problematic. Allen continually voiced the tension between the company's aesthetic commitment and the economic requirements of the music business:

> I don't know, you might get so frustrated after awhile because of economic factors. I mean, there's some very real business things. . . . We've got to get money in. People just don't buy as many records as they use to. Not only the cost, but people make cassettes. You still have to pay the same amount of money to make records and more. What it means is that people really sell a lot of very faddish and pop things. . . . It's those kinds of things that make me say I don't know. (Allen 1981)

In spite of their dislike of commercial fusion styles, Allen, Paul, and Kazuko continually debated releasing commercial fusion music as a way to manage their financial uncertainty. One group interview illustrates just how deeply they felt these tensions. Note, in particular, that the discussion of fusion focused on more than its commercial possibilities. At this point in their development Allen, Kazuko, and Paul were concerned with ways in which fusion potentially challenged their hard-won musical credibility and public identity.

> *Q:* How do you feel about releasing commercial material?
> *Allen:* Well, I guess it's one way of doing it.
> *Paul:* We've got a tape. . . . I guess you'd call it fusion. [It's] like a big band sound. You ever hear of Marvin Stamm? . . . They sent us a tape that they've done in New York and it's very interesting. It uses a synthesizer, big horns, and lots of trumpets. It's pretty good.
> *Allen:* I'm coming around to thinking, "Why not concentrate your efforts on very select people who really like what they're doing and push that." You can only do so much. We're beginning to see our limitations.

Kazuko: [To Allen] Well how do you feel about this other kind of music [fusion]?

Allen: Marvin Stamm?

Kazuko: I don't think that's selling your soul. I liked it.

Allen: That tape [Stamm] is not a fusion tape per se. . . . Marvin Stamm has very good chops.

Kazuko: He doesn't have a name.

Paul: Well, the reason that we're considering it, he doesn't have a name, but the music is so salable. It's arranged so well and it's got so much appeal that it would probably sell.

Allen: There's a couple of cuts on there, one in particular [that] have that Chuck Mangione magic. Chuck is probably a good trumpet player but he has a formula and he does something over and over in a different way. There's something about his arrangements and his playing. I like his tunes, you can hum to it and there's nothing wrong with that at all.

Paul: I think that's one place where the records are really meaningful. . . .

Allen: The thing that I don't like about Stamm a little bit is it strikes me as a bit too slick. I mean, the engineering is great but every once in awhile you hear this little click clock sound. That throws me off a little bit.[4] (Allen, Kazuko, Paul 1981)

Although it might have proved financially successful, Allen, Kazuko, and Paul felt so strongly that a fusion record was too risky in terms of their public identity that the situation with Stamm became a precedent for decisions involving music they did not like. Kazuko recalled:

We were asked if we were interested in recording this group. . . . Their spirit was wonderful. We went to hear them at Great American Music Hall. Every night they had marvelous audiences, a tremendous amount of enthusiasm, which indicated to us that it would sell. . . . I said to Allen, "What do you think? These are really nice people. Their spirit is good, what do you think." He said, "Well, I don't like the music." I didn't like it either. (Kazuko 1981)

The imbalance between their aesthetic commitment and the escalating financial costs eventually forced Allen and Kazuko to re-examine their position, but some ambivalence about the aesthetic costs of commercial success remained. As Kazuko expressed it, aesthetic priorities still governed their decisions:

We still have this problem of not being hard-headed business people. That may lead to our downfall. We feel that business is kind of nasty. The way most people make money in business is by taking advantage of other people. We do not feel it's worth continuing if we have to do that. I think that if we find that is the only way, then we'll stop. That's very idealistic, I guess. (Kazuko 1981)

And on another occasion Kazuko observed:

I'm sure these guys [owners of large, commercially successful companies] are in the music because they love the music. Otherwise, why bother? Why not sell shoes? But somehow the economics has a greater importance to them. Now, why isn't it to us? In my mind one has to make it economically so that one can survive. You're going to have to pay grocery bills, your rent, your mortgage bills, or whatever. . . . If you get too much beyond that it becomes greed. All we care about is being able to continue doing this without starving. Now to be able to own the house on Long Island or whatever, that's not it. That's not the important thing. (Kazuko 1981)

Theresa's dilemma became more acute as the company and its commitments grew. I asked Kazuko if greater attention to the business and organizational aspects of the company affected its aesthetic decisions and identity as a record company.

> *Kazuko:* It makes it more of a business whereas before it was just a lot of fun and it gave us all a lot of satisfaction. Now we have to think about it as a business..
>
> *Q:* What is it about the business dimension that you have problems with?
>
> *Kazuko:* Well, I went to a conference sponsored by *Billboard* and the people were talking about exploiting the artists and so on and to me that's a dirty word. To them it's not, because they see it as using the artists to make money. I don't think that the artist gets any more of it.
>
> *Q:* Is it possible to do all of the things that you want to do both commercially and aesthetically?
>
> *Kazuko:* I think it might be. I think it would be possible, especially since a lot of the large companies are letting people go. I mean there must be other people besides Pharoah who is disgusted with larger companies and would like to work with somebody who isn't taking advantage of them.
>
> *Q:* What is it about Theresa that makes you different?
>
> *Kazuko:* I think that it has to do with the freedom of choices. You can still let your general philosophy guide the decisions of the company. I think that with the biggies, their purpose is to make money. We feel that we have to make enough money to stay in business. but we don't have to become a multi-million-dollar corporation. That's not what we're after.
> (Kazuko 1981)

Kazuko's observations were made prior to their move to the downtown Albany office. By 1986, after a two-year stay

in the new location, where more of a business approach developed, Allen and Kazuko had changed the tone, if not the
substance, of their descriptions of the tensions between commerce and aesthetics. Allen's concern had shifted from a focus
primarily on the company's identity and integrity to concerns
about financial solvency and organizational stability. While
Allen seemed, by this point, more willing to pursue commercial material, his concern was more explicitly with the
company's ability to pursue a commercial direction and its
potential drain on resources: "You know, we're talking about
a real chancy thing. I really don't have the resources to put
into one of these commercial kinds of albums. I'm really
trying to use the stuff that I have for awhile so I can get back
on my feet financially and bring some money in and see if
we can develop other ways of selling records." (Allen 1986)

One of the ways that some of the company's resources
could be reserved and efficiently applied was either to take
on a completed project (where all Theresa would do would
be manufacture and promote the final record) or to have one
of Theresa's established artists release a commercially oriented
project. Pharoah, who had participated in several commercial
projects prior to joining Theresa, seemed open to this latter
possibility, especially if it would create record sales. Pharoah
pondered this possibility with me one July afternoon in 1986
in his Oakland, California, hotel room: "How can anyone
keep a company going without any money coming in? How
is the money spent? We've got to stop spending. The company
needs to be earning more, . . . selling more commercial stuff."
Pharoah believed that one way to manage the tensions between Theresa's aesthetic identity and this strategy of releasing commercial material was to release the commercial material

on a separate label, a division of Theresa. A separate label would allow Theresa to develop different marketing strategies and target a broader audience. Pharoah conceded that he would be willing to record commercial material as long as it was "honest and good music."

When I described Pharoah's sentiments to Kazuko and Allen, they still responded in terms of maintaining organizational resources and aesthetic integrity. Still committed to the musical vision and public identity represented in their catalogue, Kazuko noted that "his [Pharoah's] idea of commercial music is not commercial. It is a far cry from what the rest of the world means by commercial: what he means by commercial is what he hopes will make some money. That's his definition of commercial." Allen was ambivalent about Pharoah's remarks and generally concerned about the potential drain on Theresa's already strained resources.

> I know that Pharoah is interested in having the record company survive and make some money. He keeps talking about getting a record that really sells. He's talking about what I thought about, having a sublabel. I don't know how I feel about it. I don't mind a record that people feel good about if it has a commercial sound and I certainly don't mind selling like a hundred thousand [records]. I don't know. I'm open at this point. Unless it was a success I wouldn't want another division just for commercial records. I don't quite know if it's worth it or not. (Allen 1986)

Allen also believed that increased record sales and commercial visibility could be achieved not just by resorting to commercially popular materials but also by getting Pharoah more actively involved in the promotional aspects of the company.

> I kind of told him [Pharoah] this before but I don't know that I made my point. He could help out a lot more if he just made himself a lot more accessible to clients. If he really conscientiously wanted to do more playing, he's going to have to lower his price somewhat. He's got to be more accessible and let somebody else direct for awhile and I don't think he's willing to do that. (Allen 1986)

Allen's and Kazuko's willingness to entertain more commercial material that might redress the imbalance between commerce and aesthetics seems plausible because it came at a time when they were primarily concerned with the immediate stability and financial survival of the company.

Their financial stresses, distribution problems, reduced production schedule, and reduced staff made it more reasonable to consider these commercial options seriously. Ironically they considered these options within the existing aesthetic visions and public reputation of Theresa Records. Thus, by 1986 the thinking of Kazuko, Allen, and Pharoah (in contrast to their earlier positions) signaled a subtle but important aesthetic and ideological shift in their definition and management of the tensions between commerce and aesthetics.

The Expression of Independence: Illuminating Jazz

In general cultural artifacts are distinguished by their artists' imaginative use of various activities. These artists work within certain genres inventing, adopting, and experimenting with technical and aesthetic conventions (Becker 1982). For record manufacturers, genre, instrumentation, technology, packaging, and recording techniques among other things are means through which such distinctions are expressed. More to the point, a discernible style and sound are the immediate results of technical and aesthetic decisions by creative personnel as well as social judgments by noncreative personnel (Becker 1982; Kealy 1979, 1982).

Social judgments and aesthetic decisions come together, for example, when producers organize players and create situations that maximize their skill and imagination. (This is an example of Keepnews' view of the impact of the "cult of personality.") Aside from the music created in these situations, these social and sociological negotiations are important to successful recording sessions and the cultivation of a discernible sound.

For Theresa Records the sound, look, feel, and style of its music expressed significant elements of the company's stylistic directions and public identity. Together with its social organization these elements expressed Theresa's distinctive experience as an independent cultural producer. In other words, in the same sense that Gary Giddins described the independents of the 1950s as having a unique style and sound, Theresa's music, social relations, and artists convey a set of recognizable qualities.

Elements of the Theresa sound include the technical quality of the recordings and the fact that many of the recording sessions were structured around a rhythm section comprised of Idris Muhammad, Walter Booker, and John Hicks. Although these men were not, in the strict sense, the company

rhythm section, their collaborations contributed significantly
to the distinguishing sound and feeling of Theresa recordings.
These musical qualities were enhanced by an identifiable look
to the record packages, which together associated the label
and its music with a specific historical period, style, and group
of artists.[5]

For Kazuko one key to expressing Theresa's sound and
identity rested with packaging and effectively capturing on
record the feeling of the music as the members of the company
experienced it:

> To me information and communication are very important
> and I think that the cover should do what it can in that line.
> I mean the feelings and the data should be conveyed in a cover.
> I feel that way about the John Hicks LP [TR115] because I
> got a good feeling. I listened to that tape [a dinner conversation
> with John], and transcribing it, I listened to it so many times
> I really have this nice feeling about John as a person and I
> wanted to convey that. I think that it [the cover] communicates
> something about John. I mean you don't even see his face in
> one [photograph], but it's a feeling right? It's not just a record,
> not a recorded moment, but it's a feeling.[6] (Kazuko 1981)

In this passage, what Kazuko called a "feeling" describes the
meaning and experience of the people and situations that went
into the creation of the final product.

As an artifact the jazz recordings (in their package, content,
and meaning[s]) issued by an independent like Theresa expresses the company's identity, social relations, and ideology
as a cultural organization. Again, both Kazuko and Allen were
especially articulate about these experiences and how they
were captured in the music and the packaging:

Kazuko: I listened to *Rejoice* [TR112/113] and I listened to it and I saw a white light. . . . You know, that's something else that's not just music, it's this spiritualism. So, I thought, a record buyer should be buying something more than just music, you know. Because if they just want the music they can record it off the radio.

Allen: We've been talking about the need to keep the packaging thing high and even improve it. More information and more stuff that makes people wanna keep this record as a piece of history, like they keep a book. (Allen, Kazuko, Paul 1981)

As these comments indicate, Allen and Kazuko saw their music (and their experience of it) in terms that go beyond its function as a source of economic exchange. It is also clear that one of their intentions was to communicate this experience to their audience. Later in the same discussion Paul and Kazuko commented on this matter of "feeling" and the importance of communicating this to their audience. First, Paul noted, "The kind of philosophy that we have [is] to make it [music] as important as possible. It should really mean something to the artist." And Kazuko continued:

One of the things that I want to do in the packaging is to make people who buy the record feel like they were there and get to know the people. There's a picture of John Hicks at Wheeler Auditorium with these two little kids asking for his autograph and he's signing it. Include that in the package and it makes the record buyer feel that he's closer to what's going on. You know glimpses of what's really happening, not just portraits of musicians. There's more to it than just musicians; there's the whole environment. (Allen, Kazuko, Paul 1981)

There is a deliberate attempt by these producers to transcend the commodity character of their music. Some of these definitions do survive the production process, where they become part of the information that audiences use to construct meanings and interpretations for themselves. This is a central and distinguishing feature of Theresa's independent experience. It constitutes that intangible but discernible quality that defined the company and together with its structural location contributed to its independent status.[7]

The observations of Kazuko and Allen are also ideological; that is, they are self-conscious reports about their activity. Their accounts tell us what they make of their world and their work. For Allen, Kazuko, Paul, and Pharoah, Theresa's values, identity, organization, relationships, and music counted for something more significant than just selling records and maintaining financial solvency. At a more general level the comments tell us what people at this level of production in the culture industry believe it takes to continue to do their work.

Independent cultural organizations like Theresa Records operate in the seams and spaces of the modern culture industry that are vacated or ignored by conglomerates. To the extent that these firms are different in their definition and organization of their work, they are also potential sites for the production of different, even alternative, cultures. Companies like Theresa maintain flexibility and autonomy because of their social organizations and social relations, the ideologies and meanings that they develop to make sense of their work, and the absence of large, well-organized markets to which to direct their products. In how Allen, Kazuko, and Paul managed these tensions and constraints rests the lessons offered by independent cultural organizations like Theresa Records.

Theresa Records is significant for the music it represents and the organizational, ideological, and aesthetic means by which that music gets made.

AFTERWORD

Since 1986 Theresa Records has not released a major album in the United States. The company, however, remained in business. As of January 1988 Allen continued to operate the company out of his home and was still the company's primary full-time member. Although Kazuko was still involved with the company, much of her time was given to her career as a research scientist. Pharoah was still with the label in January 1988. Since 1986 he had appeared on a reunion record with Coltrane alumnus McCoy Tyner and Elvin Jones. In 1987 Pharoah released *Oh Lord, Let Me Do No Wrong* under his own name but on another independent record label, Dr. Jazz. This record did not so much mark a break with Theresa as an attempt by Pharoah to pursue other projects. As for Theresa, there were several projects in the can that Allen hoped to release sometime in 1988.

APPENDIX A

A METHODOLOGICAL NOTE

My approach to understanding Theresa placed me in the stream of the company's routine social life. I tried to get a sense of the activity that occurred in the company through interviews and first-hand observations. I observed all aspects of the company to flesh out the meanings, activity, and work that shaped its identity as an independent recording company. The explanations and understandings of its experience that I arrived at were grounded in systematic observation and careful appreciation of the company's activity.

Observational and interview data were collected over a period of fifteen months during which I alternated between regular visits and shorter periods where I did not visit at all. Throughout the fieldwork I engaged members in conversations and semi-structured interviews. Discussions and interviews were conducted with members in both individual and group settings. In all my interactions, especially conversations and interviews, my aim was to record in their own words and voices the members' account of their work.

The informal discussions formed the basis for more structured and directed questions. This informal dialogue occurred throughout all phases of the study but it was especially useful in the early stages. The more directed questions came in the middle and toward the end of the study, where they were important for fleshing out specific information. Observations took place at dinner and lunch, in the recording studio, at company meetings, in the offices, and at live performances. In some instances I alternated between being observer and participant. For example, I occasionally helped unload equipment at concerts and I sometimes offered information, comments, and advice on various situations and projects. In the initial stages of the research my activity consisted mostly of hanging out.[1]

During the various stages of the research I felt different levels of anxiety and ambivalence about my research role with the company, especially my warrant for their trust. This ambivalence and the resulting anxiety was most pronounced in the early stages of the research. As my relationship and trust with members of the company evolved, I tried to monitor their early "definition of me and my activity." I did this by attending to the quality and frequency with which they introduced me to others in the company's network and social orbit. At various concerts, for instance, Kazuko introduced me to writers, musicians, journalists, and photographers as someone observing the company and the record business.

Since the instrument for collecting and recording the data in fieldwork is the researcher, the methodological basis for theoretical claims must be subject to continual reflection and review so as to take into account how the evidence was shaped and produced. The logical relationship between the data generated in my study of Theresa is crucial to the theoretical claims I make. My initial entry into the social life of the company yielded mainly observational evidence. The type of issues I explored in the initial phase of the study were those of the "what is . . . " and "how did . . . " type and those that would help establish a warrant for my presence in the company.

Based on questions and observations in the early phases of the project, I identified categories of activity (e.g., the company's public identity, social relations, and aesthetic perspective) that proved to be central to my subsequent analysis of the company. The process by which these conceptual categories were identified was especially important to my understanding of Theresa's independent experience. My initial observations, in a sense, marked the beginnings of my theorizing about the company's activity.[2]

Fieldwork provides a useful means of understanding how small independent cultural producers and organizations structure and make sense of their work. By observing and participating in their experiences (from their vantage point), researchers can more completely understanding these companies and their products. This is especially true because much of the theoretical understanding of cultural production and organization is explained mainly in terms of structural accounts. While these variables should not be lost, they must also not blind researchers interested in culture to the rich expressions of social relations, ideology, and identity that also shape the cultural creation.

APPENDIX B

THERESA RECORDS DISCOGRAPHY

TR101:   THE BISHOP/Bishop Norman Williams (1976) (Side
          1: Figure Eight; Terry's Song; Don't Go 'Way Mad;
          Christian; Side 2: Mr. Peabody; Trane's Paradise; Ole'
          Brown)
          Personnel—Norman Williams: alto saxophone; Paul:
          piano and electric piano; Michael Formanek: electric
          bass; Obadi: drums; Allen: flugelhorn

TR102:   BISHOP'S BAG/Bishop Norman William (1978) (Side
          1: Hip Funk; One Mind Experience; Side 2: For Lee;
          Billy Ballet; Dolphy)
          Personnel—Norman Williams: alto; David Liebmann:
          tenor and soprano; Allen: fluglehorn; Paul: piano; Mike
          Clark: drums; Babatunde: congas; Michael Howell:
          guitar; Mark Williams: bass; Curtis Ohlson: bass; Clar-
          ence Bector: drums

TR103:   MUSIC FROM THE BLACK MUSEUM/Ed Kelly
          (1978) (Side 1: Museum Piece; Yesterdays; Someday;
          Side 2: Samba; Everything Must Change; Ring Shout
          Ballet)
          Personnel—Ed Kelly: piano; Smiley Winters: drums;
          Peter Barshay: bass; Willie Reeves: percussion

TR104:   IT'LL BE ALRIGHT/David Hardiman's All Stars
          (1978) (Side 1: Ape Shape; Please Send Me Someone
          to Love; Jomago; Side 2: Giant Steps; Time After Time;
          It'll Be Alright; Prime Thought)

Personnel—Bishop Norman Williams: saxophone, Joe Askew: saxophone; Leon Williams: saxophone, Sonny Lewis: saxophone; Sam Green: saxophone; Charles Hamilton: trombone; Tricky Lofton: trombone; Griggs RoAne: trombone; Al Hassan: trombone; Frank Fisher: trumpet; John Hunt: trumpet; Robert Inglemon: trumpet; Allen: trumpet; Willis Kirk: drums; James Leary: bass; Michael Howell: guitar; Randy Randolph: piano; Sweetie Mitchell: vocalist

TR105:   ONE FOR BIRD/Bishop Norman Williams (1979) (Side 1: Beth; About Time; Tahia's Outlook; Side 2: Alegra; The Doc Speaks; Koko)
Personnel—Norman Williams: alto saxophone; Paul: piano; Babatunde: drums and conga; Larry Hancock: drums; Warren Gale: trumpet; Allen, trumpet; Mark Isham: synthesizer; Marvin Williams: tenor

TR106:   ED KELLY AND FRIEND/Ed Kelly (1979) (Side 1: Pippin; Answer Me, My Love; You've Got to Have Freedom; Sweet Georgia Brown; Side 2: Rainbow Song; Newborn; You Send Me)
Personnel—Ed Kelly, piano; Pharoah Sanders: tenor and soprano sax; Peter Barshay: bass; Eddie Marshall: drums

TR107:   LEVELS OF CONSCIOUSNESS/Babatunde and Phenonmena (1979) (Side 1: Thailand Stick; Use Your Hands; Levels of Consciousness; Side 2: Thang (and I Love It); Plea from the Soul; Merely a Suggestion; It's That Simple)
Personnel—Babatunde: percussion and vocals; Muziki: piano and vocals; Marvin Boxley: electric guitar and vocals; Hiroyuki Shido: electric bass; Cedric Deombi: vocals; Jose Najera: congas; Williams Murphy: tenor saxophone and flute; Martin Fiero: alto saxophone and flute; Forest Buchtel: trumpet; with special guests: Eddie Henderson: trumpet; Julian priester: trombone; Mark Isham: synthesizer; Russell Baba: alto

TR108/109):JOURNEY TO THE ONE/Pharoah Sanders (1980)Side 1: Greetings to Idris; Docktor Pitt; Kazuko (Peace Child); After the Rain; Soledad; Side 2: You've Got to Have Freedom; Yemenja; Easy to Remember; Think About the One; Bedria)

Personnel—Joe Bonner: piano; Ray Drummond: bass; Yoko Ito Gates: koto; Eddie Henderson: flugelhorn; John Hicks: piano; Idris Muhammad: drums; Pharoah Sanders: tenor saxophone

TR110: KABSHA (1980) (Side 1: GCCG Blues; Soulful Drums; St. M; Side 2: Kabsha; I Want to Talk About You; Little Feet)

Personnel—Idris Muhammad: drums; Ray Drummond: bass; George Coleman: tenor saxophone; Pharoah Sanders: tenor saxophone

TR111: PERPETUAL STROLL/Rufus Reid (1981) (Side 1: Perpetual Stroll; Waltz for Doris; One Finger Snap; Side 2: No Place Is the End of the World; Habiba; Tricrotism)

Personnel—Rufus Reid: bass; Eddie Gladden: drums; Kirk Lightsey: piano

TR112/113: REJOICE/Pharoah Sanders (1981) (Side A: Rejoice; Side b: Highlife; Nigerian Juju Hilife; Side C: Origin; When Lights Are Low; Moment's Notice; Side D: Central Park West; Ntjilo Ntjilo/Bird Song; Farah)

Personnel—Pharoah Sanders: tenor saxophone; Joe Bonner: piano; John Hicks: piano; Art Davis: bass; Billy Higgins: drums, Elvin Jones: drums; Bobby Hutcherson: vibraphone; Babatunde: drums and percussion; Big Black: conga; Peter Fujii: guitar; Danny Moore: trumpet; Steve Turre: trombone; Lois Colin: harp; Flame Braithwaite, Sakinah Muhammad, Yevette Vanterpool, Bobby London, Carroll Scott, and George Johnson: vocals

TR114: IMPRESSIONS OF COPENHAGAN/Joe Bonner (1981) (Side 1: Impressions of Copenhagen; The North Star; I'll Say No; Side 2: Quiet Dawn; Why Am I Here?)

Personnel—Joe Bonner: piano; Paul Waburton: bass; J. Tilton Thomas: drums

TR115: SOME OTHER TIME/John Hicks (1981) (Side 1: Naima's Love Song; Mind Wine; Peanut Butter in the Desert; Ghost of Yesterday; Side 2: Some Other Time, With Malice Toward None; Dark Side, Light Side) Personnel—John Hicks: piano; Walter Booker: bass; Idris Muhammad: drums

TR116: PHAROAH SANDERS LIVE/Pharoah Sanders (1982) (Side 1: We've Got to Have Freedom; Easy to Remember; Side 2: Blue for Santa Cruz; Pharomba) Personnel—Pharoah Sanders: tenor saxophone; John Hicks: piano; Walter Booker: bass; Idris Muhammad: drums

TR117: ON THE MOVE/Nat Adderley Quintet (1983) (Side 1: Malandro; The Little Boy with the Sad Eyes; Side 2: To Wisdom the Prize; Naturally; The Scene) Personnel—Nat Adderley: trumpet; Sonny Fortune: alto saxophone; Larry Willis: piano; Walter Booker: bass; Jimmy Cobb: drums

TR118: HEART IS A MELODY/Pharoah Sanders (1983) (Side 1: Ole'; Side 2: On a Misty Night; Heart Is a Melody of Time; Going to Africa) Personnel—Pharoah Sanders: tenor saxophone; Idris Muhammad: drums; William Henderson: piano; John Heard: bass

TR119: JOHN HICKS/John Hicks (1984) (Side 1: Pas de Trois; Steadfast; For John Chapman; Star-crossed Lovers; Side 2: Lillest One of All; After the Morning; That Ole Devil Called Love; Gypsy Folk Tales) Personnel—John Hicks: piano; Olympia Hicks: piano; Bobby Hutcherson: vibraphone, Walter Booker: bass

TR120: MANHATTAN PANORAMA/George Coleman (1985) (Side 1: Mayor Koch; New York Suite; Side 2: Subway Ride; El Barrio; New York Housing Blues)

Personnel—George Coleman: tenor saxophone and vocals; Harold Mabern: piano; Jamil Nasser: bass; Idris Muhammad: drums

TR121: SHUKURU/Pharoah Sanders (1985) (Side 1: Shukuru; Body and Soul; Mas in Brooklyn; Side 2: Sun Song; Too Young to Go Steady; Jitu)

Personnel—Pharoah Sanders: tenor saxophone; Leon Thomas: vocals; William Henderson: keyboards; Ray Drummond: bass; Idris Muhammad: drums

TR122: BLUE AUTUMN/Nat Adderley Quintet (1986) (Side 1: For Duke and Cannon; The Fifth Labor of Hercules; Book's Bossa; Side 2: Blue Autumn; Tallahassee Kid)

Personnel—Nat Adderley: cornet; Sonny Fortune: alto saxophone; Larry Willis: piano; Walter Booker: bass; Jimmy Cobb: drums

TR123: JOHN HICKS IN CONCERT/John Hicks (1986) (Side 1: Some Other Time/Some Other Spring; Paul's Pal; Side 2: Pas de Trois; Say It; Soul Eyes)

Personnel—John Hicks: piano; Walter Booker: bass; Idris Muhammad: drums; Bobby Hutcherson: vibraharp; Elise Wood: flute

NOTES

CHAPTER ONE

1. The November 1987 acquisition of CBS Records by the SONY Corporation of Japan may stimulate new forms of economic integration between media and entertainment companies.

2. More aggressive promotion has also boosted general expectations among some major labels about how their jazz artists will sell. Just how far these strategies reach beyond the superstars remains to be seen.

3. Herb Wong and Orrin Keepnews, of BlackHawk and Landmark Records respectively, managed some of these problems by taking advantage of the organizational and economic resources that come from associating with a larger company. With substantial financial backing and widespread industry contacts Wong and his associates created an ambitious but well-planned organization. Keepnews linked his company with Fantasy (where Keepnews once worked as a producer) in an arrangement that gave him access to Fantasy's organizational resources, distribution machinery, and promotional expertise.

CHAPTER TWO

1. This same process occurs in other culture-producing organizations such as publishing (Powell 1979, 1982; Whiteside 1981), newspapers and magazines (Gans 1979; Tuchman 1978), and television entertainment (Cantor 1980; Gitlin 1982).

2. In many cases these decisions are based on clearly established aesthetic and professional criteria; in others gatekeepers rely on hunches, guesses, and instincts. For examples of these decision-making processes in a number of cultural organizations see Davis 1974; Ettema and Whitney 1982utlin 1983; Powell 1979; Whiteside 1981.

3. During the economic recession that hit the recording industry in the 1970s, major record companies once again began to promote and distribute records through independent wholesalers. Because of inflation and with bloated management and artist rosters, majors found some forms of independent distribution and promotion less expensive and more efficient. This process also, however, loosened the recording firms' control over key phases of the production and distribution process. As a result, there were reported increases in corruption, bribery, and payola in the recording industry. By the late 1970s and early 1980s reports of alleged corruption were so widespread that they became the focus of United States congressional investigations. Because of these suspicions, and in spite of increased costs, major firms have returned to the use of their own field personnel to distribute and promote their records.

4. I am grateful to Dr. Peter Wicke, of Humbolt University in the German Democratic Republic, for many of the ideas in this paragraph. He shared his observations with me in June 1987 during an extended research visit to the United States.

CHAPTER THREE

1. Bishop Norman Williams is a familiar figure in the San Francisco music scene both as a musician and as a founder of the One Mind Temple, a church devoted to the spiritual life and music of John Coltrane. Often misunderstood and occasionally at the center of controversy, members of the church hold religious services with Coltrane's music as a central feature. They provide food to members of the surrounding community, which is located in the Filmore district of San Francisco.

2. Pharoah appeared on some of Coltrane's most significant recordings: *Ascension* (Impulse!, 95), *Live in Seattle* (Impulse! 9202-3), *OM* (Impulse! 9140), *Meditations* (Impulse! 9110), *Cosmic Music* (Impulse 9148), *Live at the Village Vanguard Again* (Impulse! 9124), *Concert in Japan* (Impulse! 9246-2), and *Expressions* (Impulse! 9120).

CHAPTER FOUR

1. According to Brown, information on new releases is sent to Rounder Distribution's accounts every two weeks so that buyers may take their time and peruse the information at their convenience.

2. When faced with this situation some firms sever their relationships with negligent distributors and switch to major distributors or plug into a network of reliable distributors that specialize in products within a specific genre. According to both Allen and Brown, Theresa began to deal almost exclusively with distributors who specialize in jazz and who because of shared ideology and musical interest were sensitive to Theresa's specific needs and situation.

3. It is interesting to consider Allen's response to these constraints in relationship to those at other small jazz independents. For example, Orrin Keepneews at Landmark Records established a distribution deal through the larger and more resourceful Fantasy Records, where he has access to the full complement of distribution and promotional resources available to Fantasy Records. Herb Wong at BlackHawk Records operates through a network of independent distributors much as Allen does. The company's constraints associated with distribution are minimized because BlackHawk initially mounted a massive public visibility campaign to announce and introduce the company and its records in all the major jazz markets in the United States. This campaign gave the company the reputation of being stable, serious, and reputable.

CHAPTER FIVE

1. On road tours with Pharoah, Allen frequently functioned as the road manager and the producer. Kazuko's responsibilities fell more specifically in the areas of promotion and publicity. For a portion of one tour they both took on, among other things, roadie responsibilities, doing things like transporting, loading, and unloading equipment.

2. In search of a stable and reliable group of people to operate the company Allen frequently hired various friends and acquaintances to help out. For instance, prior to Paul, Allen used the consultant services of a friend to help launch the company and establish appropriate contacts in the industry. Early on he also hired personnel (art directors, photographers, an office manager) through friends' recommendations.

3. At BlackHawk Records, president and producer Dr. Herb Wong is intimately involved in all phases of the production process, especially in the conceptualization of the record jackets and the overall look of the records: "I knew many of the things that I wanted to do. I still am the guiding direction of those albums I'm involved with—placement and concept and what's important." He therefore works closely with the art director to actualize these visions (Wong 1986).

4. Although they agreed to the financial demands of the percussionist, they also agreed to discontinue working with him.

5. This possibility first came to my attention during my observations at Theresa. It was later confirmed in interviews with members of Rough Trade Records and Rhino Records. For example, after describing the formal organization of the company, a member of Rough Trade described their organization in the following terms: "We recognize other people's ability and talents. We don't fight and everybody is equal. Rough Trade works on the human side. Music is personal and work is personal. The corporate structure is a structure in title only" (Rough Trade Records 1982).

CHAPTER SIX

1. While Theodor Adorno offered sharp insights about the commodity character of popular music, his observations about jazz missed the mark widely. In his valorization of European art music and general dismissal of American popular music, Adorno failed to investigate and take seriously both the complexity and signifi-

cance of jazz in relationship to popular music and European art music.

2. I am not suggesting that this enthusiasm does not exist or is expressed differently at large major companies. See Clive Davis' account of his tenure at Columbia Records (1974).

3. It is not uncommon for headline players to hire a rhythm section of local players to play an engagement. This strategy is often cheaper (in transportation, lodging, and so on) than traveling with a working band.

4. Allen's reference to the term "slick" refers to the highly formulaic and polished rhythmic approach characteristic of a lot of fusion music.

5. See Nelson George's (1985) account of Motown Records, Peter Guralnick's (1986) inventory of various southern soul music labels, and Charlie Gillett's (1974) description of Atlantic Records.

6. Jazz fans are notorious for their compulsive regard for album jackets. Liner notes have long been regarded by jazz fans as an important source of information and critical commentary on artists, music, and developments in jazz. In this respect compact disks and cassettes are distinctly different in their meaning and the consumer's experience of them.

7. Either by mail or in person Theresa's fans and supporters frequently encouraged Allen, Kazuko, and Pharoah to continue their work. These messages were often expressed in terms that emphasized feelings, spirituality, and community. This suggested to me that audiences and consumers connected, in some significant way, with the public image projected by Theresa.

APPENDIX A

1. I use "hanging out" to connote more than merely being in the presence of group activity. It implies an active presence, attending to the activity that occurs in the social setting. In my case, this meant listening to music and engaging in conversations about

the jazz, music personalities, and significant events in the jazz culture.

2. For example, one of the characteristics that I immediately noticed was the presence of a detectable identity and unique set of social relations. I observed these qualities expressed in the recording studio, at live concerts, in meetings, and in the routine operation of the company. This excerpt from a mixing session for *Rejoice* (TR112/113), for instance, describes my early detection of these qualities: Most of the decisions regarding which songs to keep and which ones to eliminate or how bright and loud to maintain certain passages was very much the result of dialogue between Allen, Pharoah, and Mark (the recording engineer). None of the interactions I saw in the studio were hierarchical. I'm not at all sure how typical this decision-making approach is in the record business, but I think its presence at Theresa is a comment on the informal and collective relationships that exist at the company. The social relations (and ideology) at Theresa Records subsequently emerged as one of the central themes of the study. I further explored this and other conceptions by asking members of the company to describe their social relationships and what it meant to be a member of the company.

BIBLIOGRAPHY

Akey, Denise. *Encyclopedia Of Associations*, vol. 1. 16th ed. Detroit: Gale.

Allen. 1980. Interview, Berkeley, Calif.

————. 1981. Interview, Berkeley, Calif.

————. 1986. Interview, July, Berkeley, Calif.

Anderson, Perry. 1977. "The Antinomies of Antonio Gramsci." *New Left Review* 100: 5–7.

Barnouw, Erik. 1966. *A Tower in Babel. (The History of Broadcasting in the United States*, vol. 1.) New York: Oxford University Press.

————. 1975. *Tube of Plenty: The Evolution of American Television.* New York: Oxford University Press.

Baskerville, David. 1979. *Music Business Handbook Career Guide.* Los Angeles: Sherwood.

Becker, Howard. 1951. "The Professional Dance Musician and His Audience." *American Journal of Sociology*, September, pp. 136–144.

————. 1973. "Art as Collective Action." *American Sociological Review* 39: 767–776.

————. 1976. "Art Worlds and Social Types." In Richard A. Peterson (ed.), *The Production of Culture.* Beverly Hills, Calif.: Sage.

————. 1982. *Art Worlds.* Berkeley: University of California Press.

Berger, Morroe. 1947. "Jazz: Resistance to the Diffusion of a Culture Pattern." *Journal of Negro History* 32 (October): 461–494.

Billboard Publications: 1980a. *International Buyer's Guide: 1980–81* (Section 2). New York: Billboard Publications.

————. 1980b. "Many Indie Labels Reflect Healthy Music Communicty." *Billboard*, June 28, pp. S–F17.

————. 1981. "Georgia Indie Labels Loom Large in Local Talent Drive." *Billboard*, September 26.

————. 1982. "Indie Labels Declare '81 Best Year in a Decade." *Billboard*, January 16.

————. 1987. "Spotlight on Jazz." *Billboard*, June 27, pp. J1–J22.

Blum, John. 1982. "Pharoah Sanders." *Musician*, December, pp. 36–45.

Blummer, Herbert. 1969. *Symbolic Interactionism*. Englewood Cliffs, N.J.: Prentice-Hall.

Browne, Duncan. 1987. Interview, March, Cambridge, Mass.

Brower, William. 1981. "Record Review: *Perpetual Stroll.*" *Jazz Times*. Berkeley, Calif., Theresa Records Press Files.

Business Week. 1982. "A David-Goliath Threat to Cable." August 16, p. 106.

Byrd, Donald. 1978. "Music Without Aesthetics: How Some Musical Forces and Institutions Influence Change in Black Music." *Black Scholar*, July/August, pp. 9–25.

Cantor, Muriel. 1980. *Prime-Time Television: Content and Control.* Beverly Hills, Calif.: Sage.

Carey, James. 1977. "Mass Communications Research and Cultural Studies: An American View." In James Curran, Michael Gurvitch, and Janet Woollocott (eds.), *Mass Communications and Society*, pp. 409–426. Beverly Hills, Calif.: Sage.

Chapple, Steve, and Reebee Garofalo. 1977. *Rock and Roll Is Here to Pay: The History and Politics of the Music Industry.* Chicago: Nelson-Hall.

Coda. 1982. "Some Other Time by John Hicks" (record review). December 1, p. 27.

Cohen, Richard. 1981. "Small Record Companies Build on the Bay Area." *San Francisco Business Journal*, May 18, pp. 10–11.

Cole, Bill. 1976. *John Coltrane.* New York: Schirmer.

Connelly, Will. 1981. *The Musicians Guide to Independent Record Production.* Chicago: Contemporary Books.

Cooper, Allan D. 1977. "A Note on the Economic Control of Black Popular Music." *Review of Black Political Economy* 441.

Coser, Lewsi (ed.). 1978. "The Production of Culture." *Social Research* 45 (Summer): entire issue.

Cuscuna, Michael. 1984. "The Blue Note Story" (jacket liner notes). New York: Mahattan Records.

Davis, Clive. 1974. *Clive! Inside the Record Business.* New York: Ballantine.

Denisoff, R. Serge. 1975. *Solid Gold.* New Brunswick, N.J.: Transaction.

————. 1976. "Massification and Popular Music: A Review." *Journal of Popular Culture* 9, no. 4: 886–894.

Denisoff, R. Serge, and John Bridges. 1982. "Popular Music: Who Are the Recording Artists?" *Journal of Communication* 32, no. 1: 132–142.

Denisoff, R. Serge, and Richard Peterson (eds.). 1972. *Sounds of Social Change: Studies in Popular Culture.* Chicago: Rand McNally.

DiMaggio, Paul. 1977. "Market Structure, the Creative Process, and Popular Culture: Toward an Organizational Reinterpretation of Mass Culture Theory." *Journal of Popular Culture* 11: 351–362.

DiMaggio, Paul, and Paul Hirsh. 1976. "Production Organizations in the Arts." In Richard A. Peterson (ed.), *The Production of Culture.* Beverly Hills, Calif.: Sage.

Dixon, Robert M. W., and John Goodrich. 1970. *Recording the Blues.* New York: Stein and Day.

Dreyfuss, Joel. 1981. "Motown's $10 Million Gamble." *Black Enterprise Magazine*, July, pp. 26–29.

Ettema, James, and D. Charles Whitney (eds.). 1982. *Individuals in Mass Media Organizations: Creativity and Constraint.* Beverley Hills, Calif.: Sage.

Faulkner, Robert. 1971. *The Hollywood Studio Musician.* Chicago: Adline.

Feather, Leonard. 1965. *The Encyclopedia of Jazz in the Sixties.* New York: Horizon.

Foreman, Ronald. 1968. "Jazz and Race Records, 1920–32: Their Significance for the Record Industry and the Society. Ph.D. dissertation, University of Illinois at Urbana-Champaign.

Fortune. 1979. "The Record Business: Rocking to the Big Money Beat." April 28, p. 58.

Frith, Simon. 1981. *Sound Effects: Youth, Leisure, and the Politics of Rock and Roll.* New York: Pantheon.

————. 1986. "Art versus Technology: The Strange Case of Popular Music." *Media, Culture, and Society* 8: 263–279.

Gans, Herbert. 1974. *Popular Culture and High Culture*. New York: Basic Books.

———. 1979. *Deciding What's News: A Study of the CBS Evening News, NBC Nightly News, Newsweek, and Time*. New York: Pantheon.

———. 1983. "News Media, News Policy, and Democracy: Research for the Future." *Journal of Communication* 33, no. 3: 174–185.

Garofalo, Reebee. 1987. "How Autonomous Is Relative: Toward a Conception of Popular Music, Social Formation and Struggle." *Popular Music* 6 (January): 77–92.

Garofalo, Reebee, and Steve Chapple. 1980. "The Prehistory of Rock and Roll." *Radical America* 14, no. 4: 16.

Gayle, Stephen. 1982. "Solar Empire Strikes Gold." *Black Enterprise Magazine*, July, pp. 36–40.

George, Nelson. 1982. "Rapping Their Way to Gold." *Black Enterprise Magazine*, June, pp. 233–238.

———. 1985. *Where Did Our Love Go?* New York: St. Martin's.

———. 1986. "Why I Promote the Blues." *Village Voice*, August 26, pp. 74–77.

Giddins, Gary. 1986. "Impulse! Records: The Oranging of Jazz." *Village Voice*, September 9, p. 68–70.

Gillespie, Dizzy. 1979. *To Be or Not to Bop: Memoirs*. Garden City, N.Y.: Doubleday.

Gillett, Charlie. 1972. *The Sounds of the City*. New York: Outerbridge and Dienstfrey.

———. 1974. *Making Tracks*. New York: Dutton.

Gilroy, Paul. 1987. *There Ain't No Black in the Union Jack*. London: Hutchinson.

Gitlin, Todd. 1978. "Media Sociology: The Dominant Paradigm." *Theory and Society* 6: 205–253.

———. 1979a. "News as Ideology and Contested Area: Towards a Theory of Hegemony, Crisis, and Opposition." *Socialist Review* 48: 11–55.

———. 1979b. "Prime Time Ideology: The Hegemonic Process in Television Entertainment." *Social Problems* 26: 251–266.

———. 1980. *The Whole World Is Watching: Mass Media in the Making and Unmaking of the New Left.* Berkeley: University of California Press.

————. 1982. "Television's Screens: Hegemony in Process." In Michael Apple (ed.), *Cultural and Economic Reproduction in Education.* Boston: Routledge and Kegan Paul.

————. 1983. *Inside Prime Time.* New York: Pantheon.

Glaser, Barney G., and Anselm L. Strauss. 1967. *The Discovery of Grounded Theory: Strategies for Qualitative Research.* Chicago: Aldine.

Goldberg, Michael. 1982. "The Idealistic Olivia Records Hits the Ten Year Mark." *San Francisco Chronicle,* September 5, pp. 30–31.

Goodman, Fred. 1987. "Jazz Indies: While Success Today Can Be Bigger, Chainstore Bins Seem Further Away." *Billboard,* June 27, p. J6.

Gramsci, Antonio. 1971. *Selections from the Prison Notebooks.* New York: International Publishers.

Gray, Herman. 1986a. "Independent Cultural Production: The Case of a Jazz Recording Company." *Popular Music and Society* 10, no. 3: 1–17.

————. 1986b. "Social Constraints and the Production of an Alternative Medium: The Case of Community Radio." In Sandra J. Ball-Rokeach and Muriel Cantor (eds.), *Media, Audience, and Social Structure,* pp. 129–143. Newbury Park, Calif.: Sage.

Guralnick, Peter. 1986. *Sweet Soul Music.* New York: Harper.

Hall, Stuart. 1973. "Encoding and Decoding in the Television Discourse." Birmingham, Eng.: Centre for Cultural Studies, University of Birmingham. Mimeographed.

————. 1977. "Culture, the Media, and the Ideological Effect." In James Curran, Michael Gurvitch, and Janet Woollocott (eds.), *Mass Communication and Society,* pp. 315–348. Beverly Hills, Calif.: Sage.

Haralambos, Michael. 1979. *Right On! From Blues to Soul in Black America.* New York: Da Capo.

Hebdige, Dick. 1979. *Subculture: The Meaning of Style.* London: Methuen.

Hesbacher, Peter, K. Peter Etzkorn, Bruce Anderson, and David

Berger. 1978. "A Major Manufacturer's Recordings: Shifts by CBS in Artistry and Song." *International Journal of Communication Research* 4: 375.

Hirsch, Paul. 1969. *The Structure of the Popular Music Industry.* Ann Arbor, Mich.: Survey Research Center.

———. 1971. "Sociological Approaches to the Pop Music Phenomena." *American Behavioral Scientist* 14: 371–388.

———. 1972. "Processing Fads and Fashions: An Organization Set Analysis of Culture Industry Systems." *American Journal of Sociology* 77 (January): 639–659.

———. 1975. "Organizational Effectiveness and the Institutional Environment." *Administrative Science Quarterly* 20, no. 3: 327–344.

———. 1977. "Social Science Approaches to Popular Culture: A Review and Critique." *Journal of Popular Culture* 11: 2.

———. 1978. "Production and Distribution Roles Among Cultural Organizations: The Division of Labor Across Intellectual Disciplines." *Social Reserach* 45 (summer): 315–330.

Horkheimer, Max, and Theodor Adorno. 1972. "The Culture Industry: Enlightenment as Mass Deception." In Horkheimer and Adorno, *Dialectics of Enlightenment.* New York: Seabury.

Jackson, Blair. 1979. "Theresa Records: Making The Records Is the Easy Part." *San Francisco Bay Guardian*, September 6, p. 10.

Jameson, Fredric. 1979. "Refication and Utopia in Mass Culture." *Social Text* 1: 130–148.

Jay, Martin. 1974. *The Dialectical Imagination.* London: Heinemann.

Jenkins, Willard. "Record Review: *Kabsha* and *Perpetual Stroll.*" *Cleveland Jazz Report.* Berkeley, Calif.; Theresa Records Press Files.

Jones, LeRoi. 1963. *Blues People.* New York: Murrow.

Katz, Jack. 1982. "A Theory of Qualitative Methodology: The Social System Of Analytic Fieldwork." In Katz, *Poor People's Lawyers in Transition.* New Brunswick, N.J.: Rutgers University Press.

Kazuko, 1980. Interview, Berkeley, Calif.

———. 1981. Interview, Berkeley, Calif.

————. 1986. Interview, July, Berkeley, Calif.

Kealy, Edward R. 1979. "From Craft to Art: The Case of Sound Mixers and Popular Music." *Sociology of Work and Occupations* 6, no. 1: 3–29.

————. 1982. "Conventions and the Production of the Popular Music Aesthetic." *Journal of Popular Culture* 16, no. 2: 100–116.

Keepnews, Orrin. 1986. Interview, July, Berkeley, Calif.

Keepnews, Peter. 1979. "Why Big Record Companies Let Jazz Down." *Jazz Magazine*, Winter, pp. 60–64.

————. 1987. "Modern Plans for a New Era." *Billboard*, June 27, p. J1.

Kellner, Douglas. 1978. "Ideology, Marxism, and Advanced Capitalism." *Socialist Review* 42: 37–66.

Klacto Jazz Magazine. 1981. "Record Review: *Kabsha* and *Perpetual Stroll.*" June/July. Berkeley, Calif., Theresa Records Press Files.

Kofsky, Frank. 1977. *Black Nationalism and the Revolution in Music.* New York: Pathfinder.

Kreiger, Susan. 1979. *Hip Capitalism.* Beverley Hills, Calif.: Sage.

Leonard, Neil. 1962. *Jazz and the White Americans: The Acceptance of a New Art Form.* Chicago: University of Chicago Press.

Levine, Lawrence. 1977. *Black Culture and Consciousness.* New York: Oxford University Press.

Lewis, George. 1978. "The Sociology of Popular Culture." *Current Sociology* 26: 3–70.

Marcus, Greil. 1975. *Mystery Train: Images of America in Rock and Roll Music.* New York: Dutton.

Marshall, Stan. 1980. Comments at a panel discussion. Jazz Times Convention, October, Washington, D.C.

McCall, George, and J.L. Simmons (ed.). 1969. *Issues in Participant Observation.* New York: Addison-Wesley.

McDonough, Jack. 1980. "Many Indie Labels Reflect Healthy Music Community." *Billboard,* June 28.

Mills, C.W. 1959. *The Sociological Imagination.* London: Oxford University Press.

Mooney, Hugh. 1974. "Just Before Rock: Pop Music, 1950–1953 Reconsidered." *Popular Music and Society* 2: 65.

———. 1980. "Twilight of the Aquarian Age? Popular Music in the 1970s." *Popular Music and Society* 7, no. 3: 182–198.

Morse, David. 1972. *Motown and the Arrival of Black Music.* New York: Collier.

Murray, Albert. 1976. *Stomping the Blues.* New York: McGraw-Hill.

Nanry, Charles. 1972. "Jazz and All That Sociology." In Nanry, *American Music: From Storyville to Woodstock.* New Brunswick, N.J.: Transaction.

Newton, Francis. 1975. *The Jazz Scene.* New York: Da Capo.

Norman, Richman. 1980. "Max Roach Interview." *Coda* 172 (April): 4.

Paul. 1980. Interview, Berkeley, Calif.

———. 1981. Interview, Berkeley, Calif.

Penchansky, Alan. 1980. "Feminist Labels Seeking Commercial Appeal." *Billboard,* April 5, p. 3.

Peterson, Richard A. 1967. "Market Moralist and Censors of a Rising Art Form: Jazz." *Arts in Society.* 4, no. 2: 236–47.

———. 1972. "A Process Model of Folk, Pop, and Fine Art Phases of Jazz." In Charles Nanry (ed.), *American Music: From Storyville to Woodstock,* pp. 135–151. New Burnswick, N.J.: Transaction.

———. 1979. "Revitalizing the Culture Concept." *Annual Review of Sociology* 5: 137–166.

———. 1982. "Five Constraints on the Production of Culture: Law, Technology, Market, Organizational Structure, and Occupational Careers." *Journal of Popular Culture* 16: 143–153.

———. (ed.). 1976. *The Production of Culture.* Beverly Hills, Calif.: Sage.

Peterson, Richard A., and David Berger. 1971. "Entrepreneurship in Organizations: Evidence from the Popular Music Industry." *Administrative Science Quarterly* 10, no. 1: 97–107.

———. 1975. "Cycles in Symbol Production: The Case of Popular Music." *American Sociological Review* 40: 158–173.

Peterson, Richard A., and Paul DiMaggio. 1975. "From Region to

Class: The Changing Locus of Country Music." *Social Forces* 53: 497–506.

Peterson, Richard A., and Howard White. 1979. "The Simplex Located in Art Worlds." *Urban Life* 10: 2–24.

Pharoah. 1986. Interview, July, Oakland, Calif.

Powell, Walter. 1979. "The Blockbuster Decade: The Media as Big Business." *Working Paper* (July/August): 26–36.

———. 1982. "From Craft to Corporations." In James Ettema and D. Charles Whitney (eds.), *Individuals in Mass Media Organizations: Creativity and Constraint*. Beverley Hills, Calif.: Sage.

Priestley, Brian. 1982. *Mingus: A Critical Biography*. New York: Da Capo.

Raddue, Gordon. 1981. "Jazz Gems on Theresa." *Richmond Independent*, March 22. Berkeley, Calif., Theresa Records Press File.

Rapaport, Diane. 1979. *How to Make and Sell Your Own Record*. New York: Quick Fox.

Reisman, David. 1950. "Listening to Popular Music." *American Quarterly* 2: 359–371.

Rothenbuhler, Eric W., and John Dimmick. 1982. "Popular Music: Concentration and Diversity in the Industry, 1974–1980." *Journal of Communication* 32, no. 1: 143–149.

Rothschild-Whitt, Joyce. 1979. "The Collectivist Organization: An Alternative to Rational Bureaucratic Models." *American Sociological Review* 44: 509–552.

Rough Trade Records. 1982. Interview with staff members, October, San Francisco, Calif.

Rounder Distribution. 1986. "Alpha-Numerical Catalogue." Cambridge, Mass. July.

Ryan, John. 1985. *The Production of Culture in the Music Industry*. Lanham, Md.: University Presses of America.

Ryan, John, and Richard A. Peterson. 1982. "The Product Image: The Fate of Creativity in Country Music Songwriting." In James Ettema and D. Charles Whitney (eds.), *Individuals in Mass Media Organizations: Creativity and Constraint*, pp. 11–32. Beverly Hills, Calif.: Sage.

Sacks, Leo. 1981. "Not All Glad Tidings at NAIRD." *Billboard*, June 20.

———. 1982a. "New Life for NAIRD: Indie Distributors Agree." *Billboard*, June 13, p. 3.

———. 1982b. "Small Indie Label Woes Aired at NAIRD Confab." *Billboard*, June 19, p. 3.

Salaam, Yusef A. 1978. "Money Management and All That Jazz." *Black Enterprise Magazine*, December, pp. 45–47.

Sanders, Clinton. 1982. "Structural Features and Interactional Features of Popular Culture Production: An Introduction to the Production of Culture Perspective." *Journal of Popular Culture* 16: 66–75.

Santosuosso, Ernie. 1986. "His Day Job Helps Support a Record Label." *Boston Globe*, September 3, p. 54.

Selznick, Phillip. 1949. *TVA and the Grass Roots: A Study in the Sociology of Formal Organizations*. Berkeley: University of California Press.

Shaw, Arnold. 1978. *Honkers and Shouters: The Golden Years of Rhythm and Blues*. New York: Collier.

Shaw, Greg. 1982. "Independent America: An Introductory Essay." *New York Rocker*, May, pp. 17–19.

Shemel, Sidney, and William Karasilovsy. 1971. *This Business of Music*. New York: Billboard.

Simpkins, C.O. 1975. *Coltrane: A Biography*. New York: Herndon House.

Sippel, John. 1982. "Indie Distributors Flex Their Muscle." *Billboard,* April 10, p. 10.

Southern, Eileen. 1971. *The Music of Black Americans*. New York: Norton.

Sutherland, Sam. 1982. "The Indies Are Comming!" *High Fidelity*, August, pp. 68–71.

Thomas, J.C. 1975. *Chasin' The Trane*. Garden City, N.Y.: Doubleday.

Tolbert, Charles, P. M. Horan, and E. M. Beck. 1980. "The Structure of Economic Segmentation: A Dual Economy Approach." *American Journal of Sociology* 85: 1095.

Toop, David. 1984. *The Rap Attack!* Boston: South End.

Tuchman, Gaye. 1974. *The TV Establishment*. Englewood Cliffs, N.J.: Prentice-Hall.

──────. 1978. *Making News: The Social Construction of Reality*. New York: The Free Press.

──────. 1983. "Consciousness Industries and the Production of Culture." *Journal of Communication* 33, no. 3: 330–342.

Ullman, Michael. 1981. "Pharoah Sanders Takes Flight Again." *Boston Phoenix,* September. Berkeley, Calif., Theresa Records Press File.

Walton, Ortiz. 1972. *Music: Black, White and Blue*. New York: Murrow.

Warner Communications. 1978. *The Prerecorded Music Market: An Industry Survey*. New York: Warner Communications.

──────. 1980. *The Prerecorded Music Market: A Two Year Update*. New York: Warner Communications.

Weber, Max. 1947. *Theory of Social and Economic Organization*. New York: Oxford University Press.

Whiteside, Thomas. 1981. *The Blockbuster Complex*. Middletown, Conn.: Wesleyan University Press.

Williams, Raymond. 1976. "Developments in the Sociology of Culture." *Sociology* 10: 497.

──────. 1977. *Marxism and Literature*. London: Oxford University Press.

Willis, Paul. n.d. "A Theory for the Meaning of Pop Music." Unpublished paper. Birmingham, Eng.: Centre for Contemporary Cultural Studies, University of Birmingham.

──────. 1978. *Profane Culture*. London: Routledge and Kegan Paul.

Wilmer, Valerie. 1980. *As Serious as Your Life: The Story of the New Jazz*. Westport, Conn.: Lawrence Hill.

Wong, Herb. 1986. Interview, August, San Francisco, Calif.

INDEX

A & M Records, 5
ABC/Impulse!, 10. *See also*
 Impulse! Records
About Time Records, 12
Adams, Pepper, 46, 47
Adderley, Cannonball, 87
Adderley, Nat, ix, 60; Quin-
 tet, 61
Adorno, Theodor, 117
Aesthetic identity; problems
 of, 123–130
Allen, responsibilities of, x,
 xi, 93
American Society of Com-
 posers, Artists, and Pub-
 lishers (ASCAP), 25
Arista Records, 4, 50
Atlantic Records, 88

Babatunde, 43, 46, 52, 57
Barshay, Peter, 44
Beatles, 26
Bee Hive Records, 12
Benson, George, 6
Berger, David, 32, 64
Bishop, The, 38–39, 43
Bishop's Bag, 39, 42–44, 47
Black Americans, vii
Black Hawk Records, 11, 18
Black Saint Records, 11
Blue Autumn, 61
Blue Note Records, 26, 88

Bonner, Joe, 53, 56, 57, 59–
 60
Booker, Walter, 60, 131
Boone, Pat, 26
Boston Phoenix, 53
Broadcast Music Incorporated
 (BMI), 25
Brower, W. A., 56
Browne, Duncan, 67–79

Cables, George, 60
Caliman, Hadley, 43
Carter, Benny, 57
Carter, Betty, 88
CBS Records, 4, 5, 6. *See
 also* Columbia Records
Charles, Ray, 3
Clark, Mike, 43
Cobb, Jimmy, 60
Coleman, George, ix, 55, 61;
 relationship to Theresa, 98
Coleman, Ornette, 39
Colin, Lois, 57
Coltrane, John, 38, 57; rela-
 tionship to Pharoah, 49
Columbia Records, 26–27,
 36. *See also* CBS Records
Commercial success, aesthetic
 costs of, 126–130
Community, jazz, 91
Companies, big vs. small,
 31–36